# *In* PURSUIT *of* ELEGANCE

# In Pursuit of Elegance

## Why the Best Ideas Have Something Missing

### MATTHEW E. MAY

BROADWAY BOOKS
*New York*

Published in the United States by Broadway Books, an imprint of
the Crown Publishing Group, a division of Random House, Inc.,
New York.
www.broadwaybooks.com

BROADWAY BOOKS and its logo, a letter B bisected on the
diagonal, are trademarks of Random House, Inc.

All trademarks are the property of their respective companies.

Library of Congress Cataloging-in-Publication Data

May, Matthew E.
In pursuit of elegance : why the best ideas have something missing /
Matthew E. May. — 1st ed.
p.   cm.
Includes bibliographical references and index.
ISBN 978-0-385-52649-4
1. Creative ability.  2. Symmetry.  3. Planning.  I. Title.
BF408.M329 2009
153.3'5—dc22
2008041812

PRINTED IN THE UNITED STATES OF AMERICA

1  3  5  7  9  10  8  6  4  2

First Edition

# Contents

CONTENTS

While brevity may not cause elegance, longwindedness certainly prevents it. In that spirit, here is a 140-character foreword. Why 140 characters? Because that's the limit of a Twitter "tweet."

*"Less is the new more." Easy to learn: symmetry, seduction, subtraction, and sustainability. Very valuable to do. Step 1: Read Matt's book!!*

Guy Kawasaki
Author of *Reality Check* and
cofounder of Alltop.com

# The Missing Piece

O N SUNDAY, JUNE 10, 2007, nearly twelve million television viewers in the United States tuned their sets to HBO to watch the final episode of the hit series *The Sopranos*. The show, which told the story of a modern-day mob boss who runs a colorful crew of only slightly organized criminals in northern New Jersey, had garnered more than twenty major awards over an eight-year period spanning six seasons, including both the Golden Globe for Best Television Series and the Emmy for Outstanding Drama Series. Flush with acclaim previously enjoyed only by network shows, *The Sopranos* touched off a renaissance of innovative television, positioning HBO at the forefront of the entertainment industry.

The last episode held the promise of being particularly special, as creator David Chase would act as both writer and director—something of a rare event since the early days of the show in 1999. Television hadn't seen such ballyhoo and buildup since the *Friends* finale in 2004. Media critics heralded the end of an era, loyal followers expressed their sadness on their blogs and Web pages, and even the highly respected editorialist Peggy Noonan devoted her entire weekend Declarations column in the *Wall Street Journal* to the show that (violence and criminal behavior notwithstanding) had so poignantly captured the challenges everyone faces in work and life. In her words, "*The Sopranos* wasn't only a great show or even a classic. It was a masterpiece, and its end Sunday night is an epochal event."

As the hour played out that Sunday evening, everyone waited with anticipation to find out the fate of Tony Soprano. Debates had been raging for the twenty-two months since Chase had announced the final airdate: *Would he or wouldn't he be "whacked"?* But instead of receiving a concrete answer to the big question, viewers sat shocked as, during the final seconds of the show, their television screens suddenly went black. Credits rolled within a few more seconds, and *The Sopranos* series came to an end.

What is so fascinating about the abrupt ending is not the decision itself, although it was unprecedented and broke new ground artistically. Rather, what is most intriguing about the black screen is the thinking behind how it came to be and the aftermath.

The most immediate reaction—*What just happened to my television signal?*—had nothing to do with the story line, but instead rested on the assumption of electronic failure. Now, such a response may have been predictable in this age of satellite and cable TV, but what is so curious is that everyone had the *same* reaction: something had gone wrong. Only when the credits rolled and viewers realized that what they had just experienced was actually the ending did they stop and think. And it's what occurred over the course of the next few days that's worth noting.

The following Monday morning media coverage was over-whelming, with every major news source weighing in, from the *New York Times* to CNN. Critics, of course, cried foul and accused David Chase of avoidance, gimmickry, and ulterior motives. (Whatever fate Tony Soprano met would inevitably disappoint some portion of the audience, and ambiguity left open the option for a feature film.) Comedy shows like *The Daily Show* immediately mocked the event and imitated the act on their own programs. On the viewer side of the street, though, the initial bitter disappointment at being left hanging was quickly replaced by an unparalleled level of postshow scrutiny coupled with a fresh appreciation for "the genius of David Chase," spurred by his semi-cryptic public comment that "Anybody who wants to watch it, it's all there."

Realizing that every scene was carefully crafted by Chase, viewers, aided by their TiVo recorders, reexamined the show frame by frame, noting both blatant and subtle visual clues, soundtrack hints, veiled dialogue, past-show references—even nuances like camera angles, color palettes, and lighting effects. Theory upon theory popped up in both online and traditional media. The debate took on a life of its own. View-ers crafted their own endings, filling in the missing scene with the intricate trail of code Chase had provided. To most, Tony Soprano's fate became quite obvious, albeit only through a full retrospective. From the initial uncertainty, at least three different but distinct endings emerged, each with its own camp of believers arguing vehemently for their version.

The point here is that no straightforward conclusion would have engaged viewers with the same intensity and de-bate. Even if they didn't like it, most critics labeled the final airing of *The Sopranos* as the creative highpoint of the 2007 season, with many hailing it the most innovative and memorable hour in recent television history. By all accounts, the episode is quite indelible.

But what was the magic behind such dramatic and enduring impact?

The answer to that question may lie in an unexpected place: the words of Chinese philosopher Lao Tzu:

> *Thirty spokes share the wheel's hub,*
> *It is the centre hole that makes it useful.*
> *Shape clay into a vessel,*
> *It is the space within that makes it useful.*
> *Cut doors and windows for a room,*
> *It is the holes which make it useful.*
> *Therefore profit comes from what is there,*
> *Usefulness from what is not there.*

David Chase's groundbreaking choice to abandon a conventional story resolution certainly granted him the creative freedom to solve several difficult character and plot problems at once with a single stroke. Not only could he tie together seemingly disparate story lines and random scenes, but he deftly sidestepped disappointing a significant share of the audience while achieving even greater viewer involvement. The deeper thought and meticulous attention to detail required to embed subtle clues in every scene pushed him to elevate his art. The utter simplicity of the *nothingness* of that black screen exacted stunning power—it riveted and seduced the viewer. By leaving the conclusion open-ended, and thus open to interpretation, Chase engaged his audience in an entirely original and altogether different way, one that told his viewers that he respected *their* intelligence and creativity.

Was the last episode of *The Sopranos* perfect? No. "Perfection" implies something finished, something flawless. The show was anything but! It was, however, something perhaps even more powerful. It was *elegant*.

*a.*

Gaze at the image below for a moment. The three sets of right-angled lines depict something so ubiquitous that you'd be hard-pressed to make it through the day without it. Can you identify it?

If you can't, it's because a key piece of information is missing. Once that information is shared, however, you will never again be able to see the image in quite the same way again. *You are looking at the uppercase version of the most widely used letter in the English language.* The letter, though, exists in the white space. Do you see it now? It is the letter *E*. Look again. My guess is that from now on, you'll have difficulty *not* seeing it.

What you've just experienced is the power of "the missing piece." It's not a parlor trick. It's an example of the transformative idea that lies at the heart of elegance, and at the center of this book: what *isn't* there can often trump what *is*.

Just as no traditional conclusion to *The Sopranos* series

could have caused such a stir, no "complete" *E*, no matter how elaborately or ornately rendered, could have engaged you as fully and had the same kind of indelible impact on you. Once you were given a clue, your brain created the image for you, changing your mind-set, without your having much say in the matter. Like *The Sopranos* finale, the incomplete *E* took on a new form, a life of its own—one with real staying power.

What is important to take away from this quick demonstration is that the full power of elegance is achieved when the maximum impact is exacted with the minimum input. Adding anything to the figure would have actually detracted from the desired effect: the surprise you likely experienced when the *E* became visible. The *E* is obvious only in retrospect, but it is the unusually simple yet thoughtful construction of what *is* there that gives the missing piece its surprising power. Elegance is not, in other words, a matter of simple erasure.

The power of the missing piece—Lao Tzu's *what is not there*—is exactly what David Chase tapped into, consciously or not, with his final episode of *The Sopranos*. Chase did what the best innovators and most prolific individuals are doing in many different domains: creatively engaging people's imaginations by leaving out the right things.

Although this is not necessarily a new idea (Lao Tzu's wisdom is easily over 2,500 years old), it remains rare and radical nonetheless. If I asked you to tell me what the easiest thing to do in any situation might be, you might naturally and instinctively reply, with a nonchalant shrug of the shoulders, "Nothing." But doing nothing isn't easy. In fact, it's just the opposite of what comes most naturally and instinctively.

Suppose, for example, you're on an African photo safari and are just about to click the perfect shot of a mother hippopotamus and her calf when she decides to charge. If you're like most people, you'd run so fast the cheetahs would be jealous—and yet, *National Geographic* adventure journalist Boyd Matson told me that even if you can run the hundred-yard dash in nine seconds flat, that's exactly what you *shouldn't* do. And he should know—charging mama hippos are part of a day's work for Boyd. As Boyd suggests, you should stand perfectly still—in other words, *do nothing*. But that's hardly easy when an angry two-ton beast is barreling toward you.

Moreover, if I told you to do nothing for the next five minutes, my bet is you couldn't—you would undoubtedly do *something* during that time. What we normally think of as the easiest thing in the world to do—*nothing*—is in reality often the hardest.

## *b.*

The value of what *isn't* there dawned on bestselling business author and self-employed professor Jim Collins when, in the throes of his early post–Stanford Business School career at Hewlett-Packard, his favorite former professor reproached him for a lack of discipline. An expert in creativity and innovation, she told him his hard-wired energy level was riding herd over his mental clarity, enabling a busy yet unfocused life. Her words rang true: at the time, Jim was aggressively chasing his carefully set stretch goals for the year, confident in his ability to accomplish them. Still, his life was crowded with the commotion of a fast-tracking career. Her comment made him pull up short and reexamine what he was doing. To help, she did what great teachers do, constructing a lesson in the form of an assignment she called "20-10": *Imagine that you've just inherited $20 million free and clear, but you only have 10 years to live. What would you do differently—and specifically, what would you stop doing?*

The exercise did precisely what it was intended to do—make Jim stop and think about what mattered most to him. It was a turning point, for three reasons. First, he realized he'd been racing down the wrong track spending enormous energy on the wrong things. In fact, he woke up to the fact that he hated his job. He promptly quit and headed back to Stanford to launch a new career of research, teaching, and writing.

Second, the assignment became a constant reminder of just how important and precious his time is. He now starts each year by choosing what *not* to do, and each of his to-do lists always includes "stop-doing" items. Collins preaches his practice, impressing upon his audiences that they absolutely must have a "stop-doing" list to accompany their to-do lists. As a practical matter, he advises developing a strong discipline around first giving careful thought to prioritizing goals and objectives, then eliminating the bottom 20 percent of the list . . . forever.

Third, the strategy helped him identify what factors led the companies he was studying to become "great" while others remained merely "good." The great companies routinely eliminated activities and pursuits that did not significantly contribute to the following criteria: profit, passion, and perfection. Profit meant engaging in only the activities that would result in value for both the company and the customer. Passion meant having a sense of noble purpose beyond just making money. And perfection meant focusing on flawlessly executing each task in such a way as to make the competition irrelevant. All three criteria had to be met in order for any activity to remain in these great companies' repertoires.

Jim Collins made the "stop-doing" argument in an eloquent essay, which appeared in *USA Today*:

> A great piece of art is composed not just of what is in the final piece, but equally what is not. It is the discipline to discard what does not fit—to cut out what might have already cost days or even years of effort—that distinguishes the truly exceptional artist and marks the ideal piece of work, be it a symphony, a novel, a painting, a company, or most important of all, a life.

*c.*

Collins's statement came as a thunderbolt of insight for me. At the time, I was a hired gun at Toyota, struggling with a unique but challenging assignment: to identify and then teach the hidden process behind Toyota's uncanny ability to successfully implement several hundreds of thousands of inventive ideas each year. It occurred to me as I read the essay that each of those ideas had behind it the "stop-doing" philosophy.

I suddenly realized that I had been looking at the problem in the wrong way. As is natural and intuitive, I had been looking at what to *do*, rather than what to *not do*. But as soon as I shifted my perspective, the vaunted Toyota Production System became for me a study of what *wasn't* there, and of how and what to *stop doing*. The Lexus line of cars, which had by then become America's leading luxury nameplate, was suddenly a shining example of eliminating anything that lacked passion and perfection. The singular thought that what *isn't* there can often be as or more powerful than what *is* presented me with a completely different view of the world. In fact, it presented an altogether unique reality—and a life-changing one, at that.

My fresh perspective led to my authoring a book entitled *The Elegant Solution*, which used Toyota as the door through which one could walk to discover a fundamentally different view of innovation. But Toyota's world dominance resulted in what I saw as the real story being upstaged by the example. The elusive nature of elegance, and the power of elegant solutions of all kinds, remained to be explored and revealed, untethered from any single illustration.

So what I did next was apply the "stop-doing" strategy to my own life, leaving my management consulting practice behind in order to focus on writing, teaching, and conducting independent research on the hows and whys of elegance. For two years I dug deeper into the concept, trying to understand it better, looking for more stories of people and groups achieving far more with much less. It turns out that if you know where to look and what to look for, the letter *E*–type strategy at the heart of elegance can be found in a wide universe of fields: from the arts to athletics, from industry to architecture, from science to society.

I'll introduce you to some of the individuals, teams, and companies that have become adept at exploiting this uniquely powerful principle to better sculpt their ideas, performances, and lives. The point of my quest is to answer a single question: *What can we discover and learn that might allow us to bring more elegance into our own endeavors?* I should warn you in advance that the search will be exemplary rather than exhaustive—for as Henry David Thoreau once observed, if you're familiar with a principle you don't have to be familiar with all of its applications. My goal is not to reduce the concept of elegance to a stepwise prescription. There is no magic elixir, there are no secret ingredients—because there is no single recipe for elegance.

Why is elegance so surprisingly powerful? The reasons aren't readily apparent, but if we can somehow decode them, we can hope to understand the thinking required to give the phenomenon genuine utility. In other words, I'm after the bigger picture, the bigger idea.

This perspective is an admittedly Eastern view, a cultural artifact resulting from my earlier immersion in an Asian company and culture. But there is some science behind this, as well. When psychologists at the University of Illinois showed a picture of an elephant in a jungle to a study group consisting of people of all ages from the United States and Asia, the image triggered different brain activity as shown by functional magnetic resonance imaging (fMRI). Basically, for all the Americans, the part of the brain that recognizes objects was lit up. Not so for the Asians. In other words, Asians saw a jungle that happened to have an elephant in it. But the Americans saw an elephant without taking much notice of the jungle. In my pursuit of elegance, I will be focusing on the jungle that happens to have elephants in it, as opposed to examining elephants of any particular kind.

To paint that bigger picture vividly we need to examine elegance from a number of different angles. (Artists tell me this helps to "render the truth.") We need some understanding of the virtues and dimensions of elegance in order to decipher its code. We need to understand why its impact is so forcefully seductive. We need to grasp the subtractive process behind its power. We need a sustainable way to apply the insight we gain. Finally, we need an understanding of why elegant ideas are so hard to come by, what the obstacles are to crafting an elegant this or that. These few objectives will help us unwrap the central idea, and will form the basic structure of this book.

*d.*

But why, you might still be wondering, is this so important? Because a world in which *not doing* can be more powerful than *doing* is a different world than the one we are used to, with important implications. Because the most pressing challenges facing society are in urgent need of sustainable solutions—*elegant* ones. Because without a new way of viewing the world we will most assuredly succumb to employing the same kind of thinking that created so many of our problems in the first place. Because precious resources such as land, labor, and capital are at all-time premiums, and in some cases are rapidly shrinking or being depleted. Because by nature we tend to add when we should subtract, and act when we should stop and think. Because we need some way to consistently replace value-destroying complexity with value-creating simplicity. Because we need to know how to make room for more of what matters by eliminating what doesn't.

We all reach for elegance at some level, and yet it so often exceeds our grasp. Just why that's so is what I want to explore.

# CHAPTER ONE

## *Elements of Elegance*

I N THE AUTUMN of 2000, two enterprising Harvard University undergraduates, Anthony Delvecchio and Jason Karamchandari, launched a Web site they called ShuttleGirl. The concept could not have been more simple: help their classmates make sense out of the comprehensively confusing campus shuttle schedule. On the site, the two gents quipped:

> It is needless to say that taking the shuttle can be a routine part of a Harvard student's life. ShuttleGirl wants to make this aspect of your life a bit easier. Think about it. We've all seen the shuttle schedule. We've all seen twenty-year-olds reduced to tears when they board a Quad-bound shuttle at 10:00 PM only to hopelessly return to the Science Center at 10:25 PM, a final pre-Quad stop. Indeed, the shuttle schedule is complex in its organization. Some would even say that a working knowledge of game theory is necessary to

understand the current shuttle schedule. ShuttleGirl
has seen all this pain and she will stand silently no
more.

To Delvecchio and Karamchandari, and to the entire
shuttle-going student population, for that matter, the campus shuttle schedule was an incomprehensible, incomplete,
inconvenient, inaccessible, inaccurate, infuriating mess. Their
thought was to deliver just enough information, just in time,
in just the right way so that the shuttle rider's experience
would be effortless.

In addition to providing route information, ShuttleGirl
evolved to provide a number of services, including real-time
updates that could be received on cellular handheld devices.
Not unlike Google founders Larry Page and Sergey Brin,
Delvecchio and Karamchandari coupled their combined ingenuity with computer savvy, developed several new technologies, tied them to a powerful algorithm, and hid it behind a
spare, user-friendly interface.

They chose for their logo a tantalizing enigma: the silhou-
ette of an undisclosed celebrity pop star, which would later
be replaced by a partial photograph of a mystery coed that
in turn created a campuswide obsession over ShuttleGirl's
true identity.

Their platform was so enormously appealing that the
Massachusetts Bay Transit Authority (MBTA), Boston's mass
transportation agency, adopted it for its entire commuter rail
schedule. Soon, six other cities and a number of other col-
leges would purchase the system, and the duo formed a company called Second Kiss Wireless to market the ShuttleGirl
platform more widely.

In a June 2001 interview with the campus newspaper the

*Harvard Crimson,* Delvecchio said of ShuttleGirl's various capabilities: "One algorithm does it all. We think ShuttleGirl is an incredibly elegant solution."

At Davidson College in Charlotte, North Carolina, a course on short prose fiction taught by award-winning writer Randy Nelson begins with a peculiar assignment: using only a box of 250 toothpicks, three feet of string, and a 2.5-ounce tube of glue, each student must build a bridge at least two toothpicks high and strong enough to hold a brick. The goal, Nelson says, is for each student to come up with "an elegant solution—one that is simple, beautiful, strong and stunningly original," and one that uses "every inch of string, every drop of glue and clicks into place with the 250th toothpick." Nelson's lesson is directly applicable to good fiction, he says, which in his view must also be beautiful, original, sturdy, not require any more words than necessary, and click into place with the last word.

For six months in 1983, a lengthy political struggle involving the White House, Congress, and civil rights groups seemed likely to destroy the United States Commission on Civil Rights. The conflict was sparked by then president Ronald Reagan's precipitous nomination of three new commissioners. The act turned pending legislation intended to extend the life of the commission into a political minefield, as civil rights groups and Congress saw the independent, bipartisan nature of the commission threatened by executive interference. Both the House of Representatives and the Senate introduced resolutions calling for the commission to be reconstituted as an arm of Congress, rather than as a part of the executive branch. But Senate leadership was unsettled by the idea of a new commission in the legislative branch and balked at calling for a floor vote. Meanwhile, the House voted to deny the commission funding if it retained executive branch status. As the expiration date of the commission rapidly approached, negotiations intensified and ran around the clock. At the last possible minute, the Senate proposed a compromise: a new hybrid agency that would have a six-year term and eight commissioners—half Democrat and half Republican, four appointed by the president, two by the House, two by the Senate—who were to run staggered terms, with removal only for cause. In a single stroke, the offer effectively preserved the interests of all involved. Declared the *New York Times*: "It's an elegant solution."

The choice to use the phrase "elegant solution" implies that there is something distinctive about how each of these multifarious problems was resolved. What Delvecchio, Nelson, and the *New York Times* seem to share is the understanding that an elegant solution is in a class all its own, that what sets it apart is the unique combination of surprising power and uncommon simplicity, and that elegance entails achieving far more with much less when faced with a complex problem. Elegance is indeed a widely sought-after quality, and yet it takes many forms.

Scientists, mathematicians, and engineers search for theories that explain highly complex phenomena in stunningly simple ways. Artists and designers use white, or "negative," space to convey visual power. Musicians and composers use pauses in the music—silence—to create dramatic tension. Athletes and dancers search for maximum effect with minimal effort. In Japan, architects and martial artists pursue *shibumi*, a word appropriately without definition but meaning, very loosely translated, "effortless effectiveness." Physicians draw on the Occam's razor principle in an effort to find a single diagnosis to explain the entirety of a patient's symptoms, shaving the analysis down to the simplest explanation. Filmmakers, novelists, and songwriters strive to tell stories that seem simple but that foster multiple meanings yet achieve universal resonance.

But no matter how determinedly we pursue it, elegance is an elusive target. As a principle it resists reduction—it's difficult to decode. Perhaps that helps explain why it's rare. Experiencing elegance is nearly always profound: it gives us pause, often evoking an "Of course!"—usually accompanied by a mild slap to the forehead. It can change our view of things, often forever.

*Webster's New World Dictionary*, in an updated definition, describes elegance as "marked by concision, incisiveness and ingenuity; cleverly apt and simple, as an elegant solution to a problem." But is there a practical way to explain better what it is and isn't, what it means, and how it works?

*a.*

When you enter the office of retired professor Donald Knuth in the Stanford University Computer Sciences Department, several things strike you immediately as somewhat odd: he prefers pad and pencil over a keyboard, he works standing up, and he doesn't use e-mail. It's peculiar because Donald Knuth is none other than the father of computer science, revered by those in the know for his contributions to the field.

Knuth's love affair with computers and programming began over a half century ago, in 1957, and as mainframe computers were just emerging, "There was something special about the IBM 650," Knuth says in a memoir, "something that has provided the inspiration for much of my life's work."

By the following year Knuth had written instructional code for the IBM 650 and drafted a user manual. *CBS Evening News,* which featured one of Knuth's first programs—it was designed to compute basketball game statistics—described it as a "magic formula."

Author of *The Art of Computer Programming,* a multivolume tome that many consider to be the masterwork of the field, Knuth introduced, as one University of California professor put it, "elegance into programming," believing that computer programmers should view lines of computer code more as literature, so that people (and not simply other computers) could easily read and understand them. According to Knuth, elegant software requires programming in such a transparent way that not only can other programmers learn from it, but they can also enjoy reading it in front of the fire, "like good prose."

One of Knuth's favorite lecture topics is "solving puzzling problems." He knows he's ready to solve a problem elegantly when he can hold the answer in his head without having to write it down. Even with all of the advancement in software coding in the last fifty years, his programs remain the de facto standard for scientific publishing today.

What is Donald Knuth's definition of elegance? "Symmetrical, pleasingly memorable, spare—with the ease and immortal ring of an $E=mc^2$."

Those criteria are a bit cryptic, which perhaps isn't so surprising, given that Knuth's world revolves around a code, something that is by definition mysterious.

So what exactly does he mean?

*b.*

In 1782 a Swiss mathematician by the name of Leonhard Euler wrote about a numerical array called Latin squares. Latin squares were symmetrical grids with an equal number ($n$) of rows and columns. The only rule was that every number from 1 to $n$ had to appear exactly once in each row and column. In other words, if there were seven rows and seven columns, the numbers 1 through 7 would appear exactly once in each row and column.

Fast-forward nearly two hundred years to 1979, when Dell puzzle magazines published a numerical brainteaser they called Number Place. Indianapolis architect Howard Garnes had, in his spare time, tinkered with Euler's Latin squares to design a nine-by-nine Latin square with a new twist. He added nine three-by-three subgrids. Each could contain exactly one occurrence of all the numbers 1 through 9, in addition to the rows and columns requirement. The goal, of course, was to fill in the matrix completely. A few clues were given in the form of numbers already in place in one of the eighty-one boxes.

Shortly thereafter, in 1984, the Japanese publisher Nikoli introduced the game in its newspaper, adding yet a further twist. No more than thirty clues or "givens" were permitted, and they had to be distributed with exact mirror symmetry. Nikoli renamed the game Sudoku. It became a nationwide obsession in Japan within a few years.

In 2004, retired Hong Kong judge and puzzle fanatic

Wayne Gould made a trip to London in a successful effort to persuade the *Times* editors to print Sudoku puzzles in their paper. The *Times* introduced Sudoku as a daily feature on November 12, 2004. The craze spread to Australia and New Zealand, where newspapers like the *Daily Telegraph* and the *Daily Mail* began publishing Sudoku the following year. In July 2005, British satellite television channel Sky One launched the world's largest Sudoku puzzle, a 275-foot construction, by carving it in the side of a hill near the city of Bristol.

By the end of 2005, the World Puzzle Federation had declared Sudoku the number-one logic puzzle in the world. Today there are online versions, Sudoku radio and television shows and games, Sudoku clubs, strategy books, videos, card games, and competitions. In 2006, Italy hosted the first World Sudoku Championship, with teams from around the world participating. Being the champion in one's own country is tough enough, but the competition in these international games is even more fierce.

Will Shortz, the famed crossword puzzle editor for the *New York Times* and the only person in the world with a degree in enigmatology (the study of codes and puzzles), describes himself as a Sudoku "addict." By the end of 2006, Sudoku was a worldwide craze, with millions playing it daily.

So what is the connection between Sudoku and Knuth? I would argue that it is the elements of elegance. In keeping with Knuth's criteria, Sudoku can help us to arrive at a concise working definition of the concept.

First, in keeping with Knuth's first dimension, Sudoku is *symmetrical*, with its squares inside of squares and mirrored distribution of clues. Second, it is *seductive*—to the point of being irresistible and craze-worthy—another way to couch

Knuth's "pleasingly memorable." Will Shortz confirms that his Sudoku addiction stems from the seductive appeal of the empty squares to be filled in. It is intentionally spare, in keeping with Knuth's third dimension, through a process best described as *subtractive*. The Sudoku puzzle designer crafts a complete solution and then symmetrically subtracts filled-in squares to arrive at the starting grid, which is predominantly empty. Finally, and as a result of these first three, the game is *sustainable* in terms of both the infinite number of games that can be constructed, as well as players' interest in the game. In other words, there is an "ease and immortal ring" to it. In fact, Sudoku could not be easier to learn: you do not even need to know how to count, its one rule can be explained in a single sentence, it takes but a minute to grasp, and it is universal in nature (unlike crossword puzzles, which are knowledge-based as well as language-specific) because the numbers are just symbols. And yet, the underlying complexity behind the logic needed to solve a Sudoku puzzle can be incredibly challenging.

*Symmetry. Seduction. Subtraction. Sustainability.* These are the key elements of elegance—the laws that can help us harness the power of the missing piece.

*Symmetry* helps us solve problems of structure, order, and aesthetics. We are natural-born symmetry seekers. Most of nature, with its infinitely repeating patterns, is symmetrical. It is present in nearly every living thing, and we generally equate symmetry with beauty and balance. In fact, a number of studies have found that most people find symmetrical faces more attractive. But symmetry isn't limited to biology. Symmetry is where mathematics, nature, science, and art come together. We are adept at noticing a lack of symmetry, which is why we can exploit it to our advantage—when someone experiences a degree of *asymmetry*, they naturally want to "fill in" the obviously missing piece. It's the nature of symmetry that enables us to find solutions given only partial information. When symmetry comes into play, what appears to be missing isn't. It's at once absent, and yet present.

When, for example, *Sopranos* viewers were robbed of a standard story structure—a beginning, middle, and end—they were initially distraught. But when reassured by the story creator himself that the missing piece was "all there," they went in search of an ending—the "truth"—to restore their perceived loss of symmetry. Symmetry allowed you to complete the letter *E* earlier, and the role of symmetry in Sudoku is clear.

*Seduction* addresses the problem of creative engagement. It captivates any attention and activates any imagination. The power of suggestion is often stronger than that of full disclosure. Leaving something to the imagination, open to interpretation, creates an irresistible aura of mystery, and we are compelled to find answers. The seduction is in what we don't know. What we don't know far outweighs what we do, and we are naturally curious; we are easily drawn to the unknown, precisely because it *is* unknown. What isn't there drives us to resolve our curiosity.

The gentlemen of ShuttleGirl understood the impact of mystique. Withholding the true identity of ShuttleGirl wasn't a cheap schoolboy trick—it was a stroke of marketing ingenuity that engaged the entire student body.

Neuroscientists conducting research into positive emotional reactions have found that solving puzzles like Sudoku, and the missing *Sopranos* ending, activates the "satisfaction" center of the brain known as the striatum. The striatum is connected to parts of the frontal lobe known to be involved with directing logical thought and action toward goals. The accomplishment of "filling in" a Sudoku puzzle, or solving a whodunnit mystery, releases dopamine—a neurotransmitter long associated with pleasure and addictive behaviors. It delivers a mental "rush" that makes the player crave more. Will Shortz is in fact accurate in labeling his Sudoku habit as addictive.

*Subtraction* helps us solve the problem of economy. Doing less, *conserving,* doesn't come naturally. Humans are natural-born adders, hard-wired to push, collect, hoard, store, and *consume.* Perhaps that's why Costco is so successful—something about taking home thirty-six rolls of toilet tissue makes us feel especially secure.

And therein lies the conundrum. The same penchant we have to "fill in," to *add,* is exactly why elegance, being subtractive, is so elusive. Whether we're talking about a product, a performance, a market, or an organization, our addiction to addition results in inconsistency, overload, or waste, and sometimes all three. We all face these types of problems. It is how we handle them that enables or prevents elegance.

Do we really gain through loss? Can we actually *add* value by *subtracting?*

W. L. Gore and Associates, recognized as one of the world's most innovative companies, completely eliminated job titles and typical corporate hierarchy in order to release the creativity of its staff employees. Toyota's youth brand, Scion, refused to advertise and drastically reduced the number of standard features on its vehicles to allow ad-averse Generation Y buyers who wanted to make a personal statement to customize their cars with trendy accessories. Europe's "do nothing" default on organ donations—meaning you are an organ donor unless you opt out—results in nearly quadruple the participation seen in the United States. The British bank first direct went branchless and became the most highly recommended bank in the United Kingdom. French manufacturing company FAVI realized better employee relations when they eliminated their human resources department. Cities in Holland have eliminated traffic controls and experienced not only better traffic flow but also a significant drop in automobile accidents.

So the answer is yes. The trick is in understanding what to eliminate, and exactly how to go about it. Sustainability helps us solve that problem; it implies a process that is both repeatable and lasting. To consistently find elegant solutions, we need to alter how we approach problems, so that the principles of symmetry, seduction, and subtraction can be applied effectively, over and over again. A sustainable thinking strategy helps us to do that by giving us a process we can use and reuse to tap the power of the missing piece.

Together symmetry, seduction, subtraction, and sustainability provide a solid framework for understanding how these elements work in the pursuit of elegance. But while each plays a part, it is the *collective* execution of all four elements that determines the uncommon simplicity and surprising power we seek. Symmetry, for example, doesn't necessarily require or even imply a corresponding subtractive, spare quality. That something is subtractive or spare need not mean it's seductive. And simply because something is seductive in some way does not automatically render it sustainable; it may turn out to be a fleeting fancy. In fact, the elements of elegance can easily conflict with one another. That's one of the things that makes it so difficult to achieve. Elegance is *at once* symmetrical, seductive, subtractive, and sustainable.

It takes a blend of logic and creativity to understand how to balance the four.

*c.*

There is an old joke among economists that the solution for inflation is actually quite simple: lower the price of what you sell, and pay people less. The point of the joke, of course, is that the solution isn't a solution at all, because it ignores the complexities of a vexing problem. Unfortunately, the quip often plays out in real life. For example, in 2003, Mitsubishi Motors attempted to prop up their flagging sales in the United States with a promotion called Zero-Zero-Zero. Consumers could buy a car with no money down, no payments, and no interest for one full year. Unfortunately, the program lived up to its name: thousands scooped up the offer, driving their car for one year, but then letting the car get repossessed. Mitsubishi's losses approached a half billion dollars from the defaulted loans. The solution failed because it fell short of addressing the more complex issue of why no one was interested in buying a Mitsubishi vehicle in the first place.

When U.S. Supreme Court Justice Oliver Wendell Holmes Jr. said generations ago that "I wouldn't give a fig for simplicity on this side of complexity, but I would give my life for simplicity on the other side of complexity," he meant that to find elegance, you must appreciate, embrace, and then travel beyond complexity. When we use the word *elegant*, we're describing a solution that is as surprisingly powerful as it is uncommonly simple: it goes to the heart of a wickedly complex problem with such laser-like clarity that it leaves no doubt that the solution is the right one, or at the very least a long way down the right road. Elegant solutions solve intractable problems once and for all without causing further ones. Put another way, not everything simple is elegant, but everything elegant is simple.

Elegance is "far side" simplicity that is artfully crafted, emotionally engaging, profoundly intelligent. It should not be confused with "near side" simplicity, which stops short of confronting complexity, much like the "voluntary simplicity" movement that peaked during the 1990s in the U.S. Pacific Northwest did. In principle espousing a philosophy of more elegant living, in practice it centered more on rejecting and avoiding many of the complications of the modern world—a practice resulting for the most part in simply eliminating many of the conveniences and advantages of a rapidly advancing, technologically progressive society.

Elegance is to this sort of simplicity as chess is to checkers. Both are played on the same board, yet the first demands more strategic thinking and much deeper experience to truly master the goal of immobilizing—checkmating—a single piece, the opponent's king, in as few moves as possible. Games can go on for days, with no action for hours as the players think through their many moves and countermoves ahead. Checkers, with its mostly single-step play, is far less demanding, easier to learn, and quicker to play.

Chess masters understand the nature of complexity—that it is part of the game, and it's why they play it. The challenge and thrill lies in the endless search for ways to manage and exploit those complexities. Complexity isn't the enemy—without it they'd be playing checkers. Similarly, elegance requires the presence of complexity. In much the same way light requires darkness and trust requires uncertainty, without complexity one need not, in fact cannot, talk about elegance.

Elegance is about chess, not checkers.

## *d.*

There is a final oddity about Donald Knuth worth mentioning. He and his wife, Jill, have a peculiar and extensive photo collection of road signs. In fact, they have over eight hundred of them, from all over the United States and elsewhere. They are classified into one of ten major categories: arrows, intersections, lanes, road status, temporary, people, animals, vehicles, entrances, and weather. Each is listed with complete details of the sighting, accompanied by Global Positioning System coordinates. But that's not what makes the collection so strange. Rather, it's the fact that only diamond-shaped signs are included, and at that only the ones Knuth considers truly unique.

Why only those with a diamond shape? The answer is not so surprising. To Knuth, diamonds are the icon of elegance.

Think for a moment about diamonds. They are rare, valuable, and elegant. They are made from the incredibly simple elements, carbon (on which every living organism on earth is based) and oxygen (one of the predominant components of the air we breathe): carbon dioxide. They are formed in nature over eons and under just the right conditions—extreme heat and pressure—through a complex process that rearranges the carbon bonds in a highly organized and enormously powerful way. They are essentially transparent, not unlike Knuth's vision of what elegantly engineered computer code should look like. They can withstand and dissipate tremendous heat and pressure. They are balanced, symmetrical, and multifaceted when cut into gems. Diamonds become more valuable not by the addition of material, but by the subtraction of it—the precise cutting of a raw diamond into a brilliant and polished gem. The end result is seductive, carrying a unique power to captivate and enthrall. Diamonds, so the saying goes, are forever.

It is no mystery, then, why Donald Knuth is attracted to road signs that embody the ideal of elegance: *symmetry, seduction, subtraction, sustainability.*

We're ready to begin our journey. First stop: Symmetryville. What we find there may surprise you.

# CHAPTER TWO

# Desperately Seeking Symmetry

SCIENTISTS AND ARTISTS share a common mantra, one immortalized by the great poet John Keats, who contemplated the relationship between art and real life in his 1819 "Ode on a Grecian Urn": " 'Beauty is truth, truth beauty—that is all/Ye know on earth, and all ye need to know.'" While scientists attempt to explain real life logically, artists attempt to interpret it creatively. But they come together on the issues of beauty and truth, which share a common denominator: symmetry.

Since ancient times, symmetry has been at the heart of some of the most intriguing ideas in art and science. Long embraced by painters, sculptors, musicians, architects, and philosophers for its powerful aesthetic effects, symmetry has emerged over the course of the past century as an even more potent organizing principle in mathematics, physics, cosmology, and, more recently, society.

For most people, symmetry is synonymous with bilateral symmetry, the mirror type of reflection symmetry characteristic of living things and many geometric objects. Mention symmetry, and we immediately think of beautiful faces and delicate butterflies. If you take almost any creature great or small and reflect one half of it in a mirror, while small differences exist, the result is something nearly identical to the whole. In the case of proportionately balanced objects—squares, circles, triangles, for example—the result is *exactly* identical. Symmetry of this type is a naturally occurring phenomenon; even fossils dating back 650 million years reveal bilateral symmetry. Given the millions of cells and structures comprising a living organism and the correspondingly infinite number of possible (and probably simpler) ways to put them together, why bilateral symmetry is so prevalent in nature is one of the deepest questions of our existence.

Most people are also at least somewhat familiar with another kind of symmetry, the rotational kind of symmetry exhibited by, say, a snowflake, sphere, or starfish. In addition to its mirror-reflection symmetry qualities, if you rotate a sphere around any axis going through its center, it appears to be the same sphere. Rotate a snowflake, which typically has six almost identical points, around its center by any multiple of 60 degrees in the same plane as its points, and it remains unchanged. Turn the five points of a starfish any multiple of 72 degrees and the effect is the same. And the next time you're contemplating a "loves me, loves me not" with an English daisy, keep in mind that it doesn't matter how you rotate the flower, it looks the same.

But these are simply descriptions of different symmetrical characteristics. To get a concrete and universally applicable *definition* of symmetry, you have to look to mathematics. The best way to think about symmetry may be the way mathematician Hermann Weyl defined it in his seminal 1952 book, *Symmetry*:

"A thing is symmetrical if there is something you can do to it so that after you have finished doing it, it looks the same as before."

The palindrome "A Toyota's a Toyota," for example, is essentially symmetrical because it reads the same whether you read it backward or forward. Likewise, the expression $x3z+4xy+y3z$ is symmetrical because it stays the same mathematically when you swap the $x$ and $y$. And it's fairly easy to see how the previous examples adhere to this more precise definition. If you think about it, what Weyl's definition really says is that symmetry is more about dynamic properties of ordering, organizing, and operating than about static proportions of objects.

Scientists and artists agree that symmetry bridges any gap between the two seemingly disparate fields and holds the power to reconcile that which we normally think of as personal, emotional, and subjective—aesthetic beauty (proverbially being in the eye of the beholder)—with what we normally think of as impersonal, rational, and objective: the truth. Symmetry is such a fundamental characteristic of the natural world—of the universe as we believe it to be—and plays such a big role in whatever we think or do, that we often overlook its importance. Until it's absent.

And its absence carries significant implications for all of us, in ways you might never expect.

*a.*

Brian Greene is a physics professor at Columbia University and author of the 1999 bestselling book *The Elegant Universe.*

For him, symmetry is part of the air he breathes. Theoretical physicists like Greene talk in terms of the "beautiful" symmetries of nature, and dedicate their lives to attempting to explain the vast complexities of the universe through theories captured in equations, equations that attempt to distill the essence of the world around us into extremely simple terms. In other words, their day job is pursuing elegance. Einstein, for example, believed so strongly in his theory of general relativity—which explains the laws of gravity with what Greene calls "a deep inner elegance"—because it was "almost too beautiful to be wrong."

Aesthetic beauty plays a key role in the work of theoretical physicists for the simple reason that the theories they pursue describe realms of the universe that can't necessarily be proven experimentally, or even directly observed. That means they must consider hypotheses that are based at least in part on constructs that have some semblance to the things we actually experience around us. In other words, the theory must not only exhibit an internal logical consistency from a mathematical perspective, it must also reflect the structural beauty and elegance of the natural world. Symmetry is a fundamental part of that aesthetic sensibility.

To be symmetrical in Greene's world, a theory that mathematically defines some universal physical law can't break down when the surrounding circumstances of time or place change. It must work everywhere, without exception, and, as Greene states, "everywhen." For example, if the law of gravity only works on planet Earth, scientists would have to discard their understanding of gravity and look for a more fundamental, universal explanation for gravity's effects. In fact, the laws of gravity work the same way on the moon as they do on Earth, even though the *experience* is dramatically different. The reason you can perform a standing broad jump on the moon that would shatter every Olympic record is *not* because the laws change, it's because the value of one of the variables in the equation has changed: the mass of the moon is a fraction of the Earth's. So while the effects of the law under different variables may vary, the law itself must remain immutable.

For the last quarter century theoretical physicists have been grappling with a concept known as superstring theory (or string theory for short), which seems to offer the simplicity Holmes would die for, the unifying beauty Keats refers to, and the symmetry Knuth advocates. String theory is a way to reconcile the laws of the large—Einstein's theory of general relativity—with the laws of the small—quantum mechanics. General relativity basically says that time and space form a geometric structure that is smooth and curved, like a flowing fabric. Quantum mechanics holds that everything in the universe experiences undulations that get more unstable as the distance between things shrinks. At the very smallest scales, the turbulence is so violent that even the smooth fabric of space and time gets shredded. In other words, the two theories are at odds. For decades the proponents of each haven't been able to stand in the same room together. Now they can tentatively smile and share a sandwich without a food fight breaking out. String theory potentially explains the most complex of all systems: the universe, both big and small. And it does so in a grand unified way using a term we all know and understand: string.

But not just any string. A string so small that we may never be able to see it—a hundred billion billion ($10^{20}$) times smaller than the nucleus of an atom. A string so small we can only guess at its properties because we would need a particle accelerator a million billion times more powerful than exists today to determine them. (Physicists like to slam things together at unbelievable speeds in particle accelerators miles long in circumference because you can tell an awful lot about something from what happens when you do.) Strings that are vibrating like those on a violin or guitar, but shaped like a rubber band. Those vibrations are many and varied and are thought to actually be the fundamental component of the other subatomic particles, such as protons and electrons, that we observe. In other words, what look like different particles are in reality just different "notes" on the same fundamental string. Greene explains to us that "the universe—being composed of an enormous number of these vibrating strings—is akin to a cosmic symphony."

String theory proposes that, much like a letter of the alphabet in language, there is nothing smaller or more basic than these vibrating musical strings. String is string like a rose is a rose, and it can't be described as containing any other material. Of course, if you think about it, a rose too is really vibrations on a string.

But if you can't see these strings, and can't directly determine their actual properties, how can you be confident string theory holds water? In part through the power of symmetry: you can approximate the properties of something even if you only have partial information. Greene uses the example of the human face: even if you only have a picture of, say, the left side of it, you can construct a reasonably good semblance of the entire face (apart from some irregularity, such as a facial disfigurement). While differences certainly exist between the two sides of anyone's face, most are symmetrical enough to enable the rendering of a good likeness. As Greene suggests, this is how police artists construct a sketch of a suspect without having complete information. The same in-direct method is used all the time in science. You don't have to actually travel to distant stars and galaxies to understand their dynamics. And this is where the power of the missing piece meets up with symmetry.

To borrow Greene's illustration, suppose I tell you that a sequence of letters has been written on a slip of paper, that the sequence has exactly three occurrences of the letter *y*, and that the paper has been hidden within an envelope hermeti-cally sealed inside a mayonnaise jar left on Funk and Wagnall's porch since noon today. If I give you no more clues, there's no reliable way for you to determine the sequence unless you have a pair of those supercool X-ray glasses you could buy from the back of comic books in the good old days. The sequence of letters could be most anything—*hjuiydfgybvcxzy-werfgplk* would work just fine, as would an infinite number of other possibilities.

But now suppose that I give you two further hints. First, the hidden sequence of letters is an actual word in the En-glish language; second, it contains the smallest number of letters possible having exactly three *y*s. Now, there's only one possibility, the shortest English word containing three *y*s: *syzygy*. Ironically, the word denotes a special kind of unity.

This is exactly what I did with the letter *E* exercise, what David Chase did in the last episode of *The Sopranos*, and what Sudoku players use to successfully complete a puzzle.

String theory is so powerful primarily because the tini-est of all things is able to explain the greatest of all things in a single description that ties together the existing—and conflicting—concepts into one grand unified theory of ev-erything. In other words it is elegant, and while string theory cannot yet be empirically proven, it has kept the scientific community spellbound in pursuit of the evidence that will conclusively prove (or disprove) it, because of the symmetry it offers in uniting parts of our universe that are, at the moment, immeasurable.

That nature ensures the universality of its fundamental laws by treating every single moment in time and every single location in space identically is to the physicist the most compelling kind of symmetry. And while it's clear that a certain aesthetic sensibility plays an integral role in the work of the physicist, how does the definition of symmetry relate to the artist, whose entire life centers on aesthetics? As Brian Greene says: "Much in the same manner that they affect art, such symmetries are deeply satisfying; they highlight an order and a coherence in the workings of nature. The elegance of rich, complex, and diverse phenomena emerging from a simple set of universal laws is at least part of what physicists mean when they invoke the term *beautiful.*"

Greene's words were more prophetic than he could have realized.

*b.*

When Richard Taylor's resume crossed the desk of the search committee at the University of Oregon in the spring of 2000, his application for associate professor of physics almost landed in the trash bin. Taylor is no ordinary physicist. He is also an abstract artist, a career detail that would make most straitlaced academics look sideways at him. Taylor had left an academic career in physics at Australia's University of New South Wales in 1994 to pursue art in England's Manchester School of Art before continuing his work in physics, work that would eventually blend art with science. Richard Taylor, perhaps better than anyone, understands how the beauty of symmetry connects the disciplines of science, math, and art to each other and to the world around us. It was during his sabbatical at Manchester that he began to connect the dots.

Manchester believed in a "trial by fire" approach to painting, and one of Taylor's first assignments found him and his classmates braving the windswept desolation of northern England's Yorkshire moors for a cold week in February 1995. The assignment was simple enough: paint the landscapes. The problem was, the weather wasn't cooperating, and a winter snowstorm blowing in the first day made it impossible to paint outdoors—at least using the conventional, brush-to-canvas method. Weather forecasts predicted at least one more storm during the week, so Taylor and his mates met in the local tavern to strategize on just how they would complete the assignment. They decided to reenact the story of French painter Yves Klein, who drove from Paris to Toulouse through a thunderstorm with a blank canvas tied to the roof of his car. The rain created a water-stained pattern as he drove, and when he arrived in Toulouse, he framed the canvas, told people that nature had created the art for him, and sold it almost immediately. Taylor took things one step further.

Braving the storm, the merry band gathered large fallen tree branches and used them to fashion a wind-driven pendulum. The pendulum was then hung on a long branch which acted as a laundry line between two towers of tepeed branches. The pendulum, in other words, was free to go with the flow of the wind, acting like a big sail to catch the swirls and gusts. The motion of the pendulum would then be transferred to another part of the contraption holding paint containers, which would drip a corresponding pattern onto a canvas they had placed on the ground below. Since the constant flurries prevented them from seeing much of anything, they figured that whatever resulted from their rig should meet the course requirement—and even exceed it.

The setup was left unattended as the crew sought shelter to wait out the storms. When the weather cleared and Taylor returned to the scene, he was shocked to see that they, or rather, nature, had painted a Pollock. A *Jackson* Pollock. Or at least something that looked a lot like a Jackson Pollock. An ardent admirer of the iconoclastic Pollock, Taylor was struck by a flash of insight: Pollock's mad drippings, too, must have had a natural rhythm to them.

Richard Taylor pictured with the wind-driven pendulum on the Yorkshire moors. *Photograph courtesy of Richard P. Taylor.*

To solve the mystery of those rhythms in the art of Jackson Pollock, Taylor returned to his first field of study: physics. What he eventually discovered would stir the art world and fascinate the science community.

On August 8, 1949, *Life* magazine piqued the nation's ire in a profile piece on the emerging abstract painter Jackson Pollock by asking: "Is he the greatest living painter in the United States?" The *Life* spread was of major significance, not only because it was *the* magazine in a time before television, but also because not many people had ever heard of Jackson Pollock. So to ask whether he was the greatest painter alive was audacious and provocative. After the article, which revealed his work and technique, ran, the readership's overwhelming response to the question was a resounding "no!" In fact, many people didn't consider him a painter at all! Those familiar with his work viewed him as a "dripper" and "splatterer," but surely not a *painter*. In fact, *Life* later dubbed Pollock "Jack the Dripper."

Having made his exodus from the Manhattan art scene in the mid-1940s, Jackson Pollock worked out of a converted barn in a tiny town on the end of Long Island. It was there that he developed a new technique, one that was missing what most would have considered an important piece: the traditional (and quite European) stroke of a paintbrush. Pollock's method was primitive: pour, drip, splatter, and splash paint from a can, brush, or stick, never touching the canvas, which he placed on the floor of the studio. It appeared so easy that even a young child with no training could do it. Many of the letters pouring into *Life* magazine in protest said as much or worse, with specific references and uncomplimentary comparisons to the skills of certain primate species. Many claimed Pollock's art wasn't art at all, a sentiment that even Pollock himself on occasion seemed to concur with. Pollock's pieces had no focal point, no up or down, no perspective, no left or right. They were literally all over the place, pure chaos on canvas.

Or were they?

What Richard Taylor noticed immediately upon collecting the canvas from the Yorkshire moors that freezing day in 1995 was something that most people would have never seen, with or without a practiced eye for art: the paint patterns were not just reminiscent of a Pollock painting, they replicated the Pollock images in a very unique way, a way that only a mathematician could explain. Taylor recognized that the repetitive patterns in his canvas were *fractal*.

Fractals exhibit a special type of geometric symmetry, an infinitely repetitive, self-replicating, self-similar pattern that remains the same irrespective of the magnification scale. Fractals are the symmetrical patterns of *nature*, an order arising out of chaos, and are seen in snowflakes, ferns, roots, branches, waves, wind, clouds, coastlines, and human physiology (think dendrites, blood vessels, bronchial branches). The next time you steam up some broccoli, think about the fact that you're eating fractals—the florets, from the smallest single strand that never fails to get stuck in your front teeth during an important dinner date to the entire head you take home from the market, have a similar shape. Fractals have no up or down, no in or out, no focal point, and no left or right. And that was Taylor's first clue that Pollock's patterns might be, unbelievably, the very patterns of nature. I've included some examples of fractals and how they work on pages 44 and 45.

What's so fascinating about fractals is that things in nature that appear completely random and chaotic actually are mired in layered patterns of intricate, symmetrical design. Fractals do not emerge out of order, they arise out of *disorder*, aligned with a few extremely simple, unchanging relationship rules. These minimalistic rules create surprisingly organized structures that are indeed quite beautiful, as Brian Greene would say, and in fact provide the easiest, most effective way to use energy. For example, a tree's branches and roots, like our body's nerves and blood vessels, are organized in fractal patterns that result in highly sophisticated systems used to distribute the chemicals and nutrients they carry in the most efficient way. Fractals are, in other words, elegant.

Richard Taylor was an expert in fractals long before stumbling across a natural way to imitate Pollock at the Manchester School of Art. His scientific background was focused on electrical currents flowing through the circuits found in modern electronic gadgetry such as computers, cellular phones, and compact disc players. Electricity flows through these devices in a measurably ordered, controlled way. But as the development of nanotechnology became more applicable, Taylor and his colleagues were able to construct nano-electronic devices with circuits only a hundred times bigger than an atom. Taylor's research revealed that at this extreme microscopic scale, electricity ceases the orderly and controlled flow found at the larger scales and reverts back to natural patterns—*fractal* patterns—spreading out like the roots or branches of a tree, or like lightning. Taylor's work remains focused on understanding and harnessing the power of fractals for use in future electronic technology. But the discovery of fractals in the work of Jackson Pollock is what put Taylor on the map, and with good reason. Jackson Pollock died in 1956. Fractals were not discovered until 1975.

As Taylor revealed to me, not only is there an incredible

similarity between the fractal patterns of nature and those of Pollock's paintings, but the two creative *processes* are also quite similar. Based on his analysis of documentary films and observations of those witnessing Pollock in action, Taylor knew Pollock created a painting by first pouring streams of paint in discrete islands of trajectories distributed across the canvas, followed by longer extended trajectories that joined the islands, slowly and gradually building up layer upon layer of paint. The lines reflected his movements as he circled the canvas, rendering a two-dimensional translation of his three-dimensional motion. He would then stop work for hours or days, returning at a later time to drip more paint, a process similar to the patterned fits and starts of the winds that generated Taylor's snowstorm painting. Taylor believed Pollock wasn't just splattering paint about willynilly, but neither was he imposing measured, mathematical control over his drippings. He couldn't have been—he was moving far too fast and fluidly. And Richard Taylor set out to prove it.

Taylor's first clues were in the words of Pollock: "My concerns are with the rhythms of nature. I am nature." Pollock's images are often described as having a certain organic quality, suggesting a trait of nature. Jackson Pollock's close friend Reuben Kadish once said, "I think that one of the most important things about Pollock's work is that it isn't so much what you're looking at but it's what is happening to you as you're looking at his particular work." But what exactly does that mean? What was it about a Pollock painting that evoked an organic reaction? Was it similar to what we experience when we relax by a fire, gaze up at the stars, hear the wind rustle leaves, or listen to the waves crash on the shore?

Taylor knew that the answers must come from mathematics, the very same body of mathematics that Brian Greene and his fellow string theory physicists employed. So following his Manchester experience his next step was to head back to the laboratory. He conducted his long and involved investigation of the Pollock patterns in his spare time, using the very same analytical techniques that he used to study the fractal patterns of electricity flow in nano-electronic circuits.

To understand the relevance of what Taylor found, and to see how it might be applied in the world beyond theoretical math, science, and art, you have to know a bit about fractals, and why they are so important in the grand scheme of things.

The term *fractal* was coined in 1975 by Benoit Mandelbrot, who was at the time working for the IBM Thomas J. Watson Research Center in New York, applying mathematics to the real-world problems of economics, finance, and information technology. While Mandelbrot was the originator of the term, researchers and artists had been delving into symmetrical, self-repeating geometrical patterns for decades. In 1904, Swedish mathematician Helge von Koch developed an extremely simple curve, which became known as the Koch snowflake, thanks to its visible similarity to one. What is remarkable about the Koch snowflake is that if you zoom in on any section of it, it looks exactly like the larger section containing it. To create a Koch snowflake, all you have to do is start with a line segment of any length, replace the middle third of it with a triangle, then repeat that process in each resulting line segment. From very simple symmetrical rules you get a very aesthetically attractive object, one of immense visual complexity and one that alludes to nature.

But interestingly, until Mandelbrot came along, mathema-

## THE ART AND SCIENCE . . .

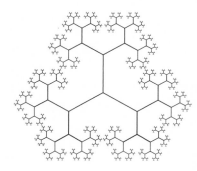

### FRACTALS

Fractals are a special type of symmetry: repetitive patterns nested within each other that remain the same at differing scales of magnification, so that the overall structure is similar to a single smaller structure. Fractals occur naturally (not as precisely as in this diagram), and arise out of very simple rules that when fed back on each other create beautifully organized and highly complex designs.

### HOW TO CREATE A KOCH SNOWFLAKE

In 1904 Helge von Koch developed a fractal curve starting with a line and replacing the middle third with a triangle. This simple algorithm, the Koch curve, is repeated endlessly. To create the Koch snowflake three Koch curves are combined.

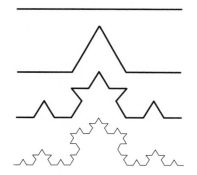

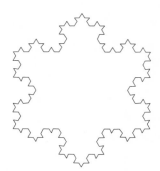

ticians, Koch included, assumed these shapes had no connection to nature. That's because nothing in nature is quite so perfect—nature likes to improvise and vary its themes, rather than repeat a pattern exactly. For example, while mountain

## ... OF FRACTALS

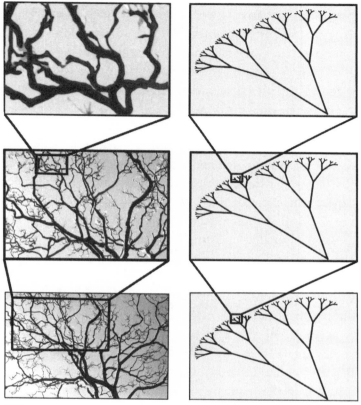

REAL TREE
Branch patterns are *statistically* self-
similar at different magnifications.

ARTIFICIAL TREE
Branch patterns are *exactly* self-
similar—identical—at different
magnifications. *Images courtesy of
Richard P. Taylor.*

ranges are considered fractal, the nooks, crags, and crannies
of a single mountain don't resemble precisely the same pattern of the entire range; but they are measurably, statistically
similar.

Mandelbrot wasn't interested in snowflakes or mountains, at least not originally. He was intrigued with the fluctuations and price variations of markets and began looking into swings in the cotton market. In 1961, he noticed something rather peculiar. What was taken for granted as random spikes and dips on a plot of any given month's prices looked eerily similar to the plot of prices over an entire decade. That led him to other, similar discoveries.

For example, a plot of the rise and fall of water levels in the Nile River over a week was similar to the plot of an entire century; the seemingly haphazard ins and outs of the British coastline were similar to the irregular profiles of single coves. Mandelbrot came by the latter discovery by asking "How long is the British coastline?" "Infinite" is the only correct answer—at smaller and smaller scales, there is always more to measure, and what's being measured is similar to the next largest scale. Mandelbrot was convinced that this similarity at different magnifications ran through all of nature, as well as through a multitude of man-made problems. He chose the term *fractal*, taken from the Latin word *fractus*, which means "interrupted" or "broken." Mandelbrot's ideas led to his 1977 book, *The Fractal Geometry of Nature*, which brought fractals into the mainstream of scientific thinking and connected nature, complexity, and startlingly simple symmetries of fractal repetition.

Today, fractals are so ubiquitous that they are called the "fingerprint of nature." And that was the framing thought in Richard Taylor's mind: Could it be possible that Pollock was able to harness and express the complex, chaotic, yet utterly pleasing aesthetics of natural fractals in the same way the wind could?

To answer the question, Taylor knew he'd need to quantify

the patterns in both his own wind-driven piece and Pollock's canvases. And to do that, he needed the help of the computer. By taking a high-resolution photograph of a painting and scanning it into a computer—a process that could take over a week at a time to perform—he was able to separate color layers and overlay a mathematical grid of identical squares, like an architect's layout pad. The computer could then analyze the contents of the squares—which had paint, which were empty, what was the pattern? The beauty of the symmetrical square grid was that you could zoom in or out to any scale, which enabled examination at any magnification. By the end of the study, Taylor had analyzed nearly 5 million patterns from twenty different Pollock drip paintings. No matter where he looked, no matter what the piece, from the smallest speck of paint to areas as large as a square meter, the patterns were fractal over the entire painting: the tiniest discernible pattern, at less than a tenth of a square inch, was more than 1,000 times smaller than the largest, up to twelve feet square in some paintings. His conclusion: *Pollock was painting fractals two decades before their discovery in nature.*

But Taylor didn't stop there. He needed to confirm whether the fractal nature of Pollock's work was what made it so appealing. If fractals were indeed the perceptual trigger, the "so what?" became that much more significant.

Taylor conducted a study on several fronts. First, he analyzed Pollock's work chronologically and computed a measure of complexity of the fractal patterns over time. That measure, or "fractal dimension," is, for two-dimensional objects, a number between 1 and 2 that denotes the level of density, and thus of the complexity, of a fractal pattern. The Koch snowflake, for example, has a complexity of 1.26. The profiles of many coastlines have a fractal dimension of around 1.45, and most natural objects when evaluated in two dimensions range between 1.2 and 1.7. Taylor found that while Pollock's work increased in complexity as time wore on—Taylor speculates Pollock was testing the limits of visual appeal—on average it corresponded to the natural range. The one and only piece falling outside the range Pollock eventually destroyed by painting over it. By analyzing a photo of the canvas taken before its destruction, Taylor was able to determine its fractal dimension: 1.9.

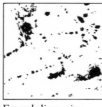
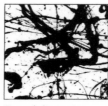

Fractal dimension of 1.1

Fractal dimension of 1.7

Fractal dimension of 1.9

*Images courtesy of Richard P. Taylor.*

That Pollock was creating fractals implied an astonishingly rare talent. Being a scientist and prone to rational explanations, Taylor thought it wise to look for a much more realistic, albeit mundane, explanation. What if Pollock wasn't doing anything intentional or special at all? What if fractals are just the accidental but inevitable result of pouring paint over a canvas? Could anyone replicate Pollock's success?

An analysis of the paint on Pollock's studio floor, paint that obviously had not quite made it to the canvas, revealed many patterns, but none were fractal. That meant that there was intentionality in Pollock's painting. But that wasn't enough. In 2004, Taylor conducted a controlled experiment with thirty-seven of his students who were asked to pour paint over canvas, Pollock-style, using art materials similar to those used by Pollock. The paintings generated were intricate, varied, and not visually unpleasant. Yet, not a single painting contained fractals.

The only way Taylor, or anyone else, could come even close to simulating Pollock's patterns naturally, without a computer, was through the use of what Taylor calls a Pollockizer, which is basically a more modern version of Taylor's wind-driven pendulum that worked so well on the Yorkshire moors. A can of paint on a pendulum is kicked into motion by electromagnetic coils near the top, and as the container moves, a nozzle at the bottom flings paint onto a piece of paper on the ground below. The size and frequency of the kick is tuned to make the motion either chaotic or regular, so the Pollockizer can generate both fractal and nonfractal patterns.

Thus, the final questions Taylor confronted were these: given the overwhelming appeal of Pollock's paintings—one of his last drip paintings, *Blue Poles,* is valued at well over $40 million—do people prefer fractal patterns over nonfractal ones? If so, does the fractal dimension range Pollock painted within, and that nature exhibits, represent some sort of ideal? If so, the implications might be enormous.

The short answer to Taylor's questions is yes. Since 2000, Richard Taylor has conducted dozens of visual perception experiments, with rather fascinating results. In a survey of 120 people to see whether fractal patterns are preferred over nonfractals, 113 people chose the fractals. In several tests involving 220 participants, subjects were shown more than forty different fractal patterns from a number of different sources. Universal preference was given to images with fractal dimensions between 1.3 and 1.5, irrespective of how the

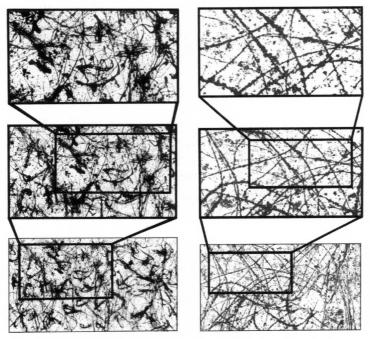

Pollock's *Number 32, 1950*: fractals          Non-Pollock drip painting: no
fractals

When a pattern is fractal, the statistical qualities repeat at finer and finer magnifications. In the painting on the right, the structure becomes diluted, loses its complexity, and the pattern looks very different at high magnification from that at low magnification. In contrast, a Pollock painting like the one on the left displays closely similar qualities at different magnifications, irrespective of size or location of the sectors chosen. In other words, the Pollock drips are fractal, while the non-Pollock drips, because they vary with pattern size, are not. *Images and analysis courtesy of Richard P. Taylor.*

THE POLLOCKIZER
Harnessing nature to capture the beautiful and complex
symmetries of the seemingly haphazard but elegantly controlled
methods of Jackson Pollock. *Photograph courtesy of Richard P. Taylor.*

fractals were generated—computer, Pollock paintings, nature photographs, or Pollockizer. Today, all of those mes-
merizing screensavers on your computer are dynamic fractals
roughly in that range.

Taylor's work proves that we are quite sensitive to the natural symmetries of fractal patterns. The question of just why
that's so hasn't been definitively answered. Taylor thinks our
appreciation, at least originally, may have had more to do with
survival than beauty. Taylor's colleague James Wise, a Washington State University associate professor of environmental
psychology, suggests the preference may have its roots in human evolution. According to Wise, our earliest ancestors on
the African plains could detect the subtle difference between
tall grass that was swayed by the wind and that which was dis-

turbed by a predator, and so be more at ease when encountering fractal patterns in the same range. But in an environment with much higher fractal density, like a rain forest, they may have been far more uneasy, alert, and vulnerable.

For our purposes we don't need to understand the precise biological mechanism responsible for our hard-wired ability to perceive these symmetries, only recognize that the strong preference exists. As they relate to the pursuit of elegance, the important lessons of fractals are these. First, extremely simple rules create surprisingly powerful outcomes. Second, the incredibly efficient self-ordering effect of adhering to these rules can achieve something far superior to anything imposed order or control can. And that has significant meaning for all of us, because whether you're talking about surviving the work world or helping the world work, effective organization is the universal challenge. It raises the question of relevance: Is it possible to achieve coordination from chaos in the real world, the world beyond theoretical physics and abstract art?

A hint for where to begin answering this question may be found in the words of Jackson Pollock himself:

> My painting does not come from the easel. On the floor I am more at ease. I feel nearer, more part of the painting, since this way I can walk around it, work from the four sides and literally be in the painting. It is only when I lose contact with the painting that the result is a mess. Otherwise there is pure harmony, an easy give and take, and the painting comes out well.

What did he mean, and how does it relate to the elegance and the world of *not doing*?

*c.*

When you approach the busy main intersection of the bustling Dutch city of Drachten, a seventeenth-century town of 45,000 in northern Holland, you quickly realize that something is dreadfully wrong. This junction is called Laweiplein by the locals and named after a *"lawei,"* an old world Netherlands device consisting of a basket hoisted high by a rudimentary wooden crane to signal peat workers when it was time to stop. Every day, some 22,000 cars travel this crossroads, along with thousands of cyclists and pedestrians. So what's wrong with Laweiplein? There is more than one missing piece. In fact, there are several.

The first thing you notice is a lack of signage or traffic lights. There is nothing whatsoever telling you to stop, slow down, or yield. The intersection is paved with red brick and forms a square roundabout. The red brick puts you on alert that something is different, and your senses heighten as you become acutely aware that there is a complete lack of definitive structure and explicit direction: there are no road divisions, no white lines, no curbs to separate cars, bikes, or people. Finally it dawns on you that what is missing is the conventional prescription for order at a traffic crossing: right-of-way.

If you were to observe the action for a few hours, you would soon see that something else associated with most intersections is also missing: obstruction. The wheeled and walking traffic through Laweiplein flows continuously in all directions across an equally shared space, and does so far better than in any traditionally controlled intersection you've ever encountered. It's not fast, but it flows—not always evenly, but naturally, like waves and wind. Between the myriad tractors, cars, trucks, lorries, bicycles, mopeds, and pedestrians, there are no horns, shouts, raised fists, squealing brakes, near-misses, or anything even remotely reminiscent of Dustin Hoffman's memorable "I'm walkin' here!!!" hood slap in *Midnight Cowboy*. What you would normally think of as flagrant right-of-way violations occur simultaneously left and right: a cyclist enters from the left and a large truck already there slows to let him pass, while an elderly woman pushes her shopping cart diagonally across the intersection without hesitation as a bus driver slows to give her wide berth. It's amazing.

Were you to actually travel through the junction, you would understand why this works so well. There is something present here that is missing from most other heavily lit, over-signaged, well-scripted intersections: immersion in, and full attention to, what's going on around you. At Laweiplein, there is great safety in danger. The question, of course, is why? The simple answer is because you must actually use your noggin. You have to slow down, and think about safety and flow. You can't *not* do that. As a traveler through Laweiplein you are not just another adherent to an imposed order, but rather a fully engaged and contributing participant in the emerging *self*-organization. Flow improves while speed slows to a natural level allowing people to make eye contact and read the situation. And that's why the traffic streams in a natural rhythm with unparalleled ease. But it didn't always. Before its complete redesign in 2004, Laweiplein was like most traffic intersections in the world—a fully regulated, fully segregated junction.

The design of Laweiplein in Drachten is an example of the vision held by Hans Monderman, a Dutch traffic investigator turned engineer. In the 1970s, Monderman began to realize through his investigation of accidents that the root cause of most incidents was that motorists are generally given far too much of exactly the wrong kind of information. According to Monderman, "Every road tells a story. It's just that so many of our roads tell the story poorly, or tell the wrong story."

For example, green lights focus all of our attention on *going*, lulling us into a robotic, one-dimensional action, reducing our peripheral attention. White lines down the center draw our attention down the road, again taking our eyes off the many potential hazards that inevitably come from the side. Red lights rob us of the opportunity to progress safely in the clear absence of danger. Monderman has said that "a wide road with many signs is basically telling you to 'go ahead, drive fast, don't worry, we have it under control for you.' That's a very dangerous message. The trouble with traffic engineers is that when there's a problem with a road, they always try to add something. To my mind, it's much better to remove things." In his view, most traffic engineers approach traffic like a sewer engineer: if you want better flow, just widen the pipe. But as roads widen, road *signs* rather than road *designs* become the mechanism to shape driver behavior.

Monderman began to realize that the generations-old philosophy of separating man and machine was inherently flawed, because it was based on an incorrect assumption, namely that *less* interaction meant *more* order. Charged with reducing speed in a small village lacking the budget to install conventional methods, on a hunch Monderman conceived a new and different approach, one completely contrary to the prevailing wisdom. His idea centered on a single, counterintuitive notion: the busier the street, the safer it becomes.

To execute his idea, Monderman removed all of the measures in place—tight S-turns, signs, lines, fencing, speed limits—leaving just the scenic village. Several months later, when Monderman returned to measure the impact, he was shocked by what he found: "When we do traditional traffic calming with speed bumps we typically expect about a 10 percent drop in speed. But with no disincentives, the speed was down by almost 50 percent, down from 57 km/hr to under 30 km/hr. I could not believe my eyes. All we had done was make a village look more like a village." This began his rather quiet war on traffic regulation, a thirtysome-year crusade the main thrust of which was to replace traffic code with social code. To Monderman, the problem wasn't one of engineering, but rather one of context.

Sadly, Hans Monderman succumbed to cancer in January 2008, before I had the opportunity to witness one of his favorite demonstrations. Monderman loved to take journalists to Laweiplein, or any one of a number of intersections he had helped design, clasp his hands behind his back, and walk straight into the flow of traffic . . . backwards. Perhaps his proudest achievement is another signature square roundabout located in the Friesland village of Oosterwolde called The Brink and known locally as Red Junction. The Brink predates Laweiplein by a half decade. Before its conversion in 1998, The Brink was a standard-issue asphalt intersection, complete with lights, lane lines, pedestrian crossings, speed postings, and right-of-way signs. Now it is a center-raised piazza paved with red brick, and *that's it.* Curbs are gone, café tables extend into the main flow, where trees have been planted. Like Laweiplein, it's marked primarily by the free flow of motorists, cyclists, and pedestrians.

In both Drachten and Oosterwolde, the impact of Monderman's design has been equally as surprising and powerful as the results of his very first experiment. Average speed, wait times, and accidents have all been cut nearly in half, and in some cases eliminated, while the overall usage and satisfaction ratings have doubled. Pedestrians and cyclists who in the past avoided these intersections altogether are now regulars. In short, things are twice as good now as they were before the conversion, with people reporting that they feel more connected to their surroundings with everyone looking out for one another.

Drachten and Oosterwolde are not just interesting anomalies. Monderman's ideas have spread to Denmark, Sweden, Belgium, Germany, France, Spain, Australia, the United Kingdom, and even the United States, with limited experiments being carried out in Florida, Massachusetts, California, and Colorado. But the full realization of Monderman's vision is nowhere in the foreseeable future.

Martin Cassini, an independent film producer in the United Kingdom and a widely recognized on-air crusader for Monderman's ideas, was quick to point out to me that eighty-plus years of the right-of-way mind-set isn't likely to change overnight. "You have to understand how traffic controls came about in the first place," he tells me. And 1929, it turns out, was a pivotal year in the history of traffic regulation.

That year a Royal Commission chaired by police commissioner Sir Henry Maybury made the distinction between major and minor roads in London, giving priority to the traveler on the main road, regardless of who'd gotten to an intersection first. This replaced the common law principle of first-come first-served, now known as filter-in-turn in the British Channel Islands, where it works well. Another rule under the main-road priority system gave priority to automobiles; if you happened to be traveling by other means, you were simply out of luck. You'd have to make a mad dash at any slim opening, however dangerous it might be. To aid the situation, formal interruptions were mandated in the form of traffic lights. Replacing the inconvenience of slowing down was the edict to stop entirely.

Nineteen twenty-nine was also the year that the planned suburban community of Radburn, New Jersey, was founded as "a town for the motor age." Radburn was designed on the view that vehicles and people should be separated. Driving and walking were completely different ways of getting around, and cars and pedestrians shouldn't share the same space. Cars received nice wide roads, people received residential "superblocks," featuring cul-de-sacs and greenbelts with paved pathways connecting the blocks. You could now send your children to school without the worry of their ever having to cross a street, and you could drive without too much concern about hitting someone. It seemed to work, and the model spread quickly on both sides of the Atlantic.

Interestingly, 1929 was also the year that Roger Morrison, a professor of highway engineering at the University of Michigan, published a paper called "The Comparative Efficiency of Stop Signs and Stop-and-Go Signals at Light-Traffic Intersections." In it, Morrison drew a compelling case against traffic lights, including, as he saw it, such negative side effects as traffic delays, the running of red lights, anger and contempt at unnecessary regulations, rear-end collisions, the speeding up to beat a yellow light, and lengthy detours to avoid lights.

Nevertheless, in 1963, the British town planner Sir Colin Buchanan issued a policy document entitled *Traffic in Towns*, formalizing the segregation principle. The result was that traffic codes were written long before much was really known about the psychology of driving behavior. The document became the forerunner of the U.K. Department of Transport's statutory *Traffic Signs Regulations and General Direction*. It is this document that Martin Cassini finds problematic, and he condemns the traffic control system for being inefficient, unsafe, vexatious, and expensive. Cassini, as Monderman did, believes self-control is the optimal control even in a metropolis like New York City or London, and he has plenty of proof to back his assertion.

On Monday, January 14, 2008, just one week after Hans Monderman's death, Cassini's *The Case Against Traffic Lights* aired on the BBC Two. One of the high points of the piece was video footage of a completely congested high-traffic intersection in London, juxtaposed with the same intersection in full flow when the lights were out due to a power failure. Interviews with cab drivers on the scene told the tale: "Traffic lights are a lot easier when the lights aren't working. So, get rid of 'em, eh?" "Whenever they're *not* working, you never get traffic. Traffic flows a bit more freely then, dunnit?" "You don't need 'em, you just have to be a bit more careful in the junction, 's all."

In an April 14, 1989, letter responding to an editorial entitled "Turn Out the Lights, and the Jam's Over" by *Washington Post* columnist "Dr. Gridlock," reader Robert Funk relayed a similar experience:

One day last week we had a power outage in parts of Fairfax County and Alexandria. All of the traffic lights were out. Well Dr. Gridlock, you would expect chaos, but instead the traffic flowed beautifully. There were no backups, people were careful and polite and I saw no accidents. Traffic from the side streets flowed into the main street on opportunity. Drivers would slow down and motion them out. Perhaps the lack of frustration from sitting at some lights for 5 to 15 minutes was responsible, who can tell? All I know is that it worked. I arrived at work a full 25 minutes ahead of my normal time. Perhaps stop and yield signs could do a better job than this complicated and expensive light system that seems to create huge backups. Perhaps it is time to rethink our traffic control system that seems to make the mess worse as time passes. I have never enjoyed my rush-hour trip as much as the day the lights went out.

Hans Monderman believed that traffic controls do not, and cannot, create that kind of behavior, but rather that you have to build it into the design of the road. As he told the *Times* in the August 22, 2004, Sunday edition: "Treat people like zombies and they'll behave like zombies. But treat them as intelligent, and they'll respond intelligently."

What Monderman is saying is exactly what Jackson Pollock was saying, only in different words: when you are fully involved in a process governed by very simple relationship rules, a natural inclination takes over, and a self-organized pattern emerges that is far more orderly than anything legislation could produce. Under those circumstances, you're connected and interacting with what's around you. Lose that connection, and a mess ensues. Hans Monderman thought that traffic controls sever us entirely from the very connections we need to travel safely and they amount to admitting defeat in achieving good road design.

That raises the most important question of all: What are the dynamics under which these natural symmetries can develop? To answer that, you would need to ask someone fortunate enough to have worked with Hans Monderman in designing shared spaces like Laweiplein in Drachten— British urban designer Ben Hamilton-Baillie.

Ben has designed a number of successful shared spaces called home zones in the U.K. The goal is to get people into the streets, because in his view, a sign warning you about children in the street is nowhere near as effective as actually *having* kids in the street. While you may glance at a sign, you essentially ignore it, especially if you've seen it before. Ben will tell you that "Research shows that over 70 percent of traffic signs are indeed ignored by motorists. But your reflex action upon seeing a child in or near the street is to exercise extreme caution." His point is that the old way of giving priority to motorists is potentially lethal. For example, if you know you have the right-of-way, and that children aren't supposed to be playing in the street in the first place, a child dashing out from the side who is worried only about retrieving her ball is a child at high risk. But without that clear separation, you have no choice but to constantly be on the alert. Like Hans Monderman, Ben says that travel controls give a false sense of security, an illusion of safety, which is "the biggest mistake we can make. Traffic rules strip us of our capacity for socially responsible behavior, our ability to be considerate. The greater the number of prescriptions, the more the sense of personal responsibility dwindles."

As Ben is fond of saying, "You don't need a sign in your living room saying 'No Spitting.' The design of your house reflects implicit values strong and clear enough to suggest appropriate behavior. In fact, if you had such a sign, it would just be distracting and counterproductive." What he means is that how we behave is ultimately governed by our surroundings and the cultural signals that go along with them. So by removing clear boundaries and blending street with sidewalk, you create a social context for behavior based on the environment itself. In a space shared equally by drivers, bikers, and walkers, the right-of-way priority disappears, replaced by good judgment and common sense in interpreting the simplest of governing core values required of any working relationship: respect for others.

I asked Ben about the first-come, first-served, filter-in-turn model that Martin Cassini mentioned works well in the Channel Islands. In Ben's view, the whole notion of first *anything* is unnecessary, because it will just lead you back to the original problem: an artificial prioritization. The use of shared space should be no different from what happens when a natural line or rhythm develops as you leave a football game or concert or go ice skating in a rink; in fact, he thinks the latter is an excellent metaphor for how things should work. "What's wrong with how we engineer things is that most of what we accept as the proper order of things is based on assumptions, not observations," Hamilton-Baillie says. "If we observed first, designed second, we wouldn't need most of the things we build." To his point, in spite of the billions spent each year around the world on installing and maintaining traffic controls, there is absolutely *no* comprehensive research anywhere to demonstrate the benefits of traffic signals—in either the context of traffic flow or safety—but there *are* a number of studies showing their detrimental effect.

To use his ice-skating rink analogy, suppose for a minute that you've never seen one, never heard of one. You arrive at the rink to see a flurry of activity: people lacing up steel blades, stepping onto a bed of ice filled with skaters gliding all about. It's a crowded field, yet somehow everyone fits. There are no lanes, but there is constant flow. Some people travel the perimeter, while others stick to the center, showing off their spins and leaps. Some are expert, some are beginners. Many travel backwards. Speeds vary. Your only thought is that this is complete madness. There is a general direction, but beyond that, you're at a loss figuring out the rules, if there are any. You're intimidated by what seems to be an utter lack of control and order. But as you keep watching, you notice that with a bit of practice, there is nothing really to worry about. There are no major accidents. Any rogue violator of the unwritten rules is quickly put straight by the masses. Speeds and shifts are dictated by the crowd skating, the overall ebb and flow begins to take on the patterns of a flock of birds in flight. You begin to understand the amazing complexity and subtlety with which people interact and communicate. If you were a Brian Greene, you'd liken it to a human particle accelerator and take note of all the little person-to-person bumps and minor collisions that relay behavior-guiding information. If you were a Richard Taylor, you'd say that what you're witnessing is an emerging fractal pattern—in other words, symmetry in motion. Finally, if you were like most people, you'd realize that there is no need to design any rules at all. Your fear would subside, confidence would build, and you'd try it, because after all, it now looks like fun.

"We have a sophisticated ability to handle complex situations far beyond what traditional engineering assumes," states Ben. "Signs and lines only inhibit the way we work as social creatures. They reduce our extraordinary ability to read and respond to situations appropriately, because the more evidence there is of legislated control, the less we think we have to be involved, to use our own senses."

Ben seeks to design an aesthetically pleasing space that encourages the kind of natural rhythms of eye contact and personal interaction you find in a skating rink. As he says in Martin Cassini's documentary film *In Your Car No One Can Hear You Scream*:

> If you remove the regulated world of signs, lines, markings, traffic signals, barriers and bollards, we start to think in the same way as if we're simply walking down the street. What shared space does is to exploit the natural skills of humans to negotiate movement, resolve conflict, and engage not only with each other but with their context. Shared space might look chaotic, but people are using their brains and intuition, not acting as mere automatons in response to signals from on high.

In every shared space he designs, Ben Hamilton-Baillie is creating a Pollock. Or, more accurately, a human-centered Pollockizer and a canvas on which a Pollock can be created. Just as Richard Taylor's Pollockizer captures on canvas the fractal patterns of nature powered by the wind, so do these shared spaces capture the deeply patterned, self-organizing behavior powered by the human intelligence. And like a Pollock painting, out of the apparent chaos springs an organic, highly desirable, most beautiful symmetry.

### d.

There are a few valuable points to take away from this short pass through the land of symmetry.

First, symmetry is a fundamental property woven into the fabric of the universe, a quality that has held the fascination of civilization since its beginning and that was present before it. From the vibrations of invisible bits of matter, to weather and other environmental conditions, to the distant galaxies, there are recurring, rhythmic, self-replicating patterns at play. Being symmetrical ourselves, inside and out, we are highly sensitive to the kind of order it creates. Symmetry helps us solve problems beyond our immediate comprehension; we know it's there, we need only discover its form. What's challenging is that symmetry isn't always readily observable, we don't always know what to look for, and we have a tendency to look at individual parts of things, rather than at larger patterns. So we are fooled into thinking we must create symmetry ourselves, usually going straight at the organizational characteristic itself rather than patiently looking for the underlying simplicity that is already in existence. Ever chasing the new idea, we apply our technological prowess to situations when, if we were instead to stop, observe, and think—to *stop doing* if only long enough to discern a repetitive pattern—we might be surprised to see that the answers lie just below the surface of what appears to be out of control. You don't need to design what already exists just because you don't immediately recognize its presence. In other words, the challenge or problem we're trying to solve might not always need our help. And if it does, understanding the power of symmetry allows us to design better, more elegant solutions.

Think about it: Is the idea of shared spaces really that radical? Only in the context of the most modern mentality. It takes but a glance at any old photograph or painting of a pre-1929 cityscape—or a quick YouTube search for "India Traffic" for that matter—with its streets jammed with all manner of vehicles and pedestrians going this way and that, to see that shared spaces are simply a step back in time to a time or place before the imposition of traffic light technology.

The second point follows from the first and is best expressed by what is known as the Montana Paradox. In December 1995, the state of Montana reverted to its pre-1975 highway speed standard of "reasonable and prudent," similar to the German Autobahn, which meant that speed limits were not based on numerical maximums, but on flow management by what motorists considered safe for the prevailing conditions. For the next five years, with no form of speed limit on its rural primary highways, Montana recorded its lowest fatality rates in twenty-five years. At the same time, however, the Montana State Police interpreted the standard in a manner inconsistent with the intent and chose to enforce ad hoc an 80–90 mph limit. During the challenge of a ticket issued for a speed over that unofficial limit, the Montana Supreme Court declared the "reasonable and prudent" standard unconstitutional on the basis of ambiguity and uncertainty. In 2000, Montana reinstituted the National Maximum Speed Limit, and that year saw a 111 percent increase in road fatalities. During the next two years, Montana recorded all-time record highs in road fatalities.

What the Montana Paradox reinforces is that by attempting to control what may already be in balance, we can inadvertently tip things the other way. In the rush to create order and organization, we often get the exact opposite of the intended, desired effect. This is the lesson of fractal symmetries—that a few simple rules are all that might be necessary to create effective, highly efficient, well-organized patterns. Elegance might best be achieved not by demanding compliance to an exhaustive set of centrally mandated, onerously rigid regulations, but from one or two vital agreements, often implicit, that everyone understands and is accountable for, yet that are left open to individual interpretation and variation, the limits of which are set by social context.

The counterintuitive dynamic at work is this: the more we try to control and regulate our risk, the more exposed and at risk we are, because the more protected from hazards we think we are, the less conscious of potential dangers we become. We actually disengage our brains and disconnect from what's happening around us. That can be disastrous. For example, you don't need driver behavior studies to tell you that if your car is fitted with better brakes, you will drive differently. You will actually drive faster and brake later. You will unconsciously convert to a performance advantage something intended to be a safety benefit. Conversely, if you've been putting off getting new brake pads and know full well your brakes are a bit of a question mark, you'll drive slower and brake sooner—which means you'll drive more safely—which are the very outcomes desired in the first place.

The implications are enormous for highly regulated environments, including government and industry. For example,

many large corporations approach high rates of absenteeism by drafting strict penalty policies. Some have gone so
far as to hire "absentee coordinators" to shadow employees,
in the belief that employees will show up if policed well.
Toyota Motor Corporation took the opposite approach
when it partnered with General Motors in 1983 to reopen a
shuttered plant, one that had been plagued with 20 percent
absenteeism and the lowest quality and productivity of all
GM's plants at the time. Inheriting the same union workforce,
Toyota reduced the more than one hundred job descriptions
to three, took more than a dozen levels of supervision down
to just a few, and embedded in the culture two crucial, nonnegotiable agreements that represent the heart and soul of
the Toyota philosophy: respect for people and continuous
improvement. Workers were placed in charge of their own
work and encouraged to interpret these ideals in their own
way. Within two years, absenteeism dropped to 3 percent,
quality and productivity rose to record highs, and the 5,000
union grievances on file were replaced by more than 15,000
employee-led improvements.

Finally, it seems safe to say that when you remove certainty
and predictability, engagement and awareness rise. The concept of shared space makes that clear. The less stated something is, the more powerful it becomes. Uncertainty and
ambiguity can create intrigue, which makes us slow down
and think. We don't immediately see the symmetry and order we so desperately seek and that transfixes our attention,
draws us in.

In 1969, the year in which he won the Nobel Prize in
Literature, Irish dramatist Samuel Beckett published a short
piece of experimental prose entitled *Sans* in French. He then

rewrote the piece in English and called it *Lessness*. It begins this way:

> Ruins true refuge long last towards which so many false time out of mind. All sides endlessness earth sky as one no sound no stir. Grey face two pale blue little body heart beating only up right. Blacked out fallen open four walls over backwards true refuge issueless.
>
> Scattered ruins same grey as the sand ash grey true refuge. Four square all light sheer white blank planes all gone from mind. Never was but grey air timeless no sound figment the passing light. No sound no stir ash grey sky mirrored earth mirrored sky. Never but this changelessness dream the passing hour.

The rather chaotic nature of the narrative actually has a great deal of order and symmetry to it, and my bet is that your brain is furiously trying to find the pattern and meaning in just these two short paragraphs. What makes *Lessness* so experimental is that Beckett used a few simple rules to randomly generate the sentences. In fact, Beckett was quite precise in creating a sense of indeterminacy. Yale University Library has on file a document in which Beckett offers a few keys to deciphering the meaning of *Lessness*. The whole piece is based on six "statement groups" of ten sentences each. These sixty sentences are presented twice, each time in a different order and paragraph structure. The paragraphs all have between three and seven sentences. Without making his overall themes explicit, Beckett gave each of the six statement groups a particular thematic element and used a formal structure, some scholars believe, to convey the arbitrary way in which we structure time (sixty minutes in an hour, twenty-four hours in a day, seven days in a week, twelve months in a year, etc.). Beckett told renowned theater scholar Ruby Cohn how he did it, and in her 1973 book *Back to Beckett,* she revealed the code:

> He wrote his sixty different sentences in six families, each family arising from an image. Beckett wrote each of these sixty sentences on a separate piece of paper, mixed them all in a container, and then drew them out in random order twice. This became the order of the hundred twenty sentences in *Sans.* Beckett then wrote the number 3 on four separate pieces of paper, the number 4 on six pieces of paper, the number 5 on four pieces, the number 6 on six pieces, and the number 7 on four pieces of paper. Again drawing randomly, he ordered the sentences into paragraphs, according to the number drawn, finally totalling one hundred twenty.

The important point is that, irrespective of whether or not *Lessness* is in fact random and chaotic, to the reader it *appears* to be so. It's the absence of obvious symmetry and clear order that engages the reader. You cannot predict what comes next, and you cannot reduce the text to a succinct, simple message. In fact, some mathematicians have determined that Beckett may have been telling readers not to attempt to reduce apparent chaos, but to accommodate it. They point to the fact that each half of *Lessness* contains 769 words, a prime number, irreducible to factors other than itself and the number I. In their paper *Lessness—Randomness, Consciousness and Meaning,* University of Dublin professors Elizabeth Drew and Mads

Haahr wrote that "The absence of an obvious determinism guiding the flow provides a gap in understanding that spurs the reader's interaction with the piece. The sense of patterning in the chaotic sequence of sentences entices the reader to untangle the random arrangement and attempt to piece together an elusive storyline."

The question now is why and how does such ambiguity and uncertainty seduce us into this sort of creative participation in the unfolding drama?

# CHAPTER THREE

## *Seduced by Nothing*

IT IS NEARLY impossible to make it through a typical day without exchanging ideas. Whether deciding on something as simple as a restaurant for a long-overdue night out or as complicated as the design of an entirely new product, we are forever involved in sculpting and selling our creative thought. Conventional wisdom says that to be successful, an idea must be concrete, complete, and certain. But the most engaging ideas are often none of those things. As the lessons of Laweiplein and Ben Hamilton-Baillie's design of high-traffic intersections show us, ambiguity and uncertainty can create compelling, intriguing, even life-saving ideas.

Seductive ideas rest on our ability to spark the kind of intrigue that will keep the imagination engaged. Not knowing exactly what's going to happen next can create a sense of suspense that keeps us glued to our seats when watching a thriller and quickly turning the pages in a mystery novel. If we can too easily guess the outcome or if the conclusion is not surprising enough we are disappointed. As soon as we become confident in our conclusion, we may lose interest entirely.

So what exactly is behind that seductive magic that draws us in, spellbinds us, and enthralls our imaginations? Where does it come from?

*a.*

In the early afternoon of November 2, 2007, I stood transfixed before the *Mona Lisa* in her permanent residence at the Louvre in Paris. In researching several different disciplines to trace the source of the magnetic pull of ambiguity and uncertainty, I had come across a statement by noted art historian E. H. Gombrich in his masterwork, *The Story of Art*, regarding Leonardo da Vinci's most famous work: "What strikes us first is the amazing degree to which Lisa looks alive. She really seems to look at us and to have a mind of her own. Like a living being, she seems to change before our eyes and to look a little different every time we come back to her. Even in photographs of the picture we experience this strange effect, but in front of the original in the Louvre it is . . . uncanny."

Truth be told, I wasn't quite getting the full impact of what Gombrich was talking about from any of the various reproductions of the *Mona Lisa* I looked at, so I traveled to the Louvre in the high hopes that I might see what he was describing. And he was right. Look once at the *Mona Lisa*, you'll find her rather sad and forlorn. Take a quick tour of the rest of the wing and come back, and now she's flirting with you. On the third turn, she's, well, downright mocking you. As

Gombrich says, "All this sounds rather mysterious, and so it is." The question is, what makes the *Mona Lisa* so magically changeable and captivating?

The grand master of using the power of uncertainty and ambiguity to create mystery and intrigue is Renaissance genius Leonardo da Vinci. And the clues to his genius—none of which involve secret societies, religious conspiracies, or codes of any kind—lie in the *Mona Lisa*. Leonardo da Vinci solved the problem facing all Florentine painters in the late 1400s: how to make a painting look alive. Until the *Mona Lisa*, even the most grand and impressive of paintings contained human figures that looked rather *in*human—more like stone statues, frozen and lifeless. Gombrich surmised that the more exactly an artist attempted to re-create the subject, copying it line by line and feature by feature, the less a viewer could imagine that it ever lived and breathed.

Leonardo da Vinci invented the technique called *sfumato*—literally "in the manner of smoke"—which he loosely defined as "without having distinct edges and lines." With *sfumato*, lines are left a little vague, and forms are slightly blurred to merge with one another. This is what allowed da Vinci to achieve such lifelike effects. The mystery of the *Mona Lisa* is somewhat less mysterious once you see that the corners of her eyes and mouth—the two features responsible for human expression—are deliberately indistinct. She seems to be alive because her attitude is so open to interpretation.

Leonardo advised aspiring painters, "paint so that a *fumoso* [smoky] edge can be seen, rather than hard and harsh outlines and silhouettes . . . that is, more confused—that is to say, less clear." In other words, Leonardo is advocating leaving something to the imagination. But why? In Gombrich's view, it is because da Vinci was aware of the superiority of tantalizing suggestion over exactitude in engaging the viewer's eye. Da Vinci instructs artists to leave any preliminary sketch indeterminate precisely because "confused shapes arouse the mind." Gombrich said that *sfumato* leads the observer "to understand what one does not see." Leaving something for us to guess at was a stroke of genius. Five centuries later, Leonardo's work continues to spawn an industry of lectures, debates, books, and movies.

But da Vinci wasn't alone in taking the road less finished. Michelangelo perfected and made famous a technique pioneered by sculptor Donatello before him, called *non finito,* meaning unfinished or incomplete. A shallow relief style, *non finito* not only left sculptures seemingly unfinished, it made them appear deeper than they actually were. Michelangelo's subjects were essentially "stuck" in the block of material, purportedly to emotionally involve the observer by revealing and preserving in stone the human artistic struggle.

But neither Leonardo nor Michelangelo was the first to explore the concept of purposefully unfinished or ambiguous work. As the Zen philosophy took hold in Japan during the twelfth and thirteenth centuries, Japanese art and philosophy began to reflect one of the fundamental Zen aesthetic themes, that of emptiness. In the Zen view, emptiness is a symbol of inexhaustible spirit. Silent pauses in music and theater, blank spaces in paintings, and even the restrained motion of the sublimely seductive geisha in refined tea ceremonies all take on a special significance because it is in states of temporary inactivity or quietude that Zen artists see the very essence of creative energy. Because Zen Buddhists view the human spirit as by nature indefinable, the power of suggestion is exalted as the mark of a truly authentic creation. Finiteness is thought to be at odds with nature, implying stagnation,

which is associated with loss of life. The goal of the Zen artist is to convey the symmetrical harmony of nature through
clearly asymmetrical and incomplete renderings; the effect is
that those viewing the art supply the missing symmetry and
thus participate in the act of creation. The famous poet Fu-
jiwara Teika developed the equivalent of *non finito* in his verse,
believing that "the poet who has begun a thought must be
able to end it so masterfully that a rich space of suggestions
unfolds in the imagination of his audience." Teika's work became a guiding force in the development of Zen thought in
Japan, and his treatises on aesthetics are viewed by historians
as the equivalent of universal handbooks on the philosophy
of art.

In Western Europe, the concept of *non finito* spread well
beyond the Italian Renaissance. In 1620, Sir Francis Bacon
worked himself into a state over what he perceived to be a
serious shortcoming of the human condition: our neglect of
absence. As Sir Francis decried in his *Novum Organum,* "by far
the greatest hindrance and aberration of the human understanding proceeds from the dullness, incompetency, and de-
ceptions of the senses; in that things which strike the sense
outweigh things which do not immediately strike it, though
they may be more important. Hence, contemplation usually
ceases with seeing, so much so that little or no attention is
paid to things invisible."

His comments may have helped to spark a new line of
thinking, for during the British Romantic period of the late
1700s, the capacity of the *non finito* to engage the beholder's
imagination became of primary interest to artists, and a
painter's preliminary sketch began to be seen as a form of art
in its own right. Irish philosopher Edmund Burke in 1757
wrote of the ability of a rough and indeterminate sketch to

stimulate the imagination "beyond the best finishing." Scottish philosopher Henry Home, Lord Kames, gave *non finito* center stage in his 1762 *Elements of Criticism,* in which he talks of Chinese gardens: "The Chinese give play to the imagination. They hide the termination of their lakes: the view of a cascade is frequently interrupted by trees, through which are seen obscurely the waters as they fall. The imagination once roused, is disposed to magnify every object."

In the late 1800s and early 1900s, French postimpressionist painter Paul Cézanne desired to engage his audience at yet another level, and used even more extreme *non finito* to render what his early detractors criticized as half-finished images. Yet Cézanne believed that thinking and imagining were the keys to truly seeing, and thought through each masterful stroke of his brush, carefully leaving out what he wished the viewer's imagination to finish.

While these are historical examples, *non finito* has made plenty of modern appearances. One vivid example (aside, of course, from *The Sopranos* finale) is the scene in Mike Nichols's 1967 classic dramedy *The Graduate,* in which young college graduate Ben Bradford (*"Mrs. Robinson, you are trying to seduce me"*), played by Dustin Hoffman, plunges into the swimming pool clad in full scuba gear, speargun and all, and remains submerged at the bottom, contemplating his so-called life. There is no dialogue, no narration, no music, only the sound of Ben's breathing. Yet because of the masterful construction of what came before in the film, we have all the context we need to interpret what the character is thinking and feeling. At the same time, the scene remains open to our interpretation, and we're allowed to inject our own personal experiences and emotions into the inaction. According to film critic Joe Morgenstern, the two-minute-long "silent" scene ranks among the most indelible and ingenious in cinema history.

It would appear that the conventional rules requiring ideas to be concrete and complete have at the very least some very noteworthy exceptions. In fact, these exceptions may not be exceptions at all. They may be the basis of new rules, rules that, like the artists and designers granting their audience a freedom to finish what the creator began, reflect the highest respect for the intelligence of others. And those are the very kinds of rules that can change the game entirely.

*b.*

On the morning of January 9, 2007, Apple CEO Steve Jobs took center stage at San Francisco's Moscone Center to deliver his keynote address kicking off the 2007 MacWorld Conference. Dressed in his signature mock turtleneck and jeans, he demonstrated the latest and greatest gizmo in Apple's product line. It was called the iPhone, and it was scheduled to go on sale five months later at the end of June. As he ticked through the features of the phone, the audience appeared mesmerized by what they saw.

And what they saw was a new gadget of remarkably sleek design, which they had come to expect from Apple. Apple's entry into the market for mobile marvels was a "smart" phone that combined cellular phone, e-mail, Internet browsing, music, photos, and video. Unlike competitive models that used limited or "light" versions of computer operating systems and Web browsers, the iPhone had the robust software of full-size Apple computers. In fact, it had full functionality across the board, including identical versions of all the features of Apple's ubiquitous mp3 player, the groundbreaking iPod. By all accounts, the iPhone was a thing of beauty, a piece of art, and irresistibly seductive.

But while the iPhone dazzled the audience, it was what they *didn't* see that took them by surprise, and even shocked them. Apple lovers had become accustomed to Jobs's flare for spare. They knew that minimalism, especially relating to buttons, was his obsession. The keyboard for the original Macintosh had no direction keys for the cutsor. Until 2005, the Mac mouse had only one button, rather than the traditional two of most computers; Mr. Jobs had long criticized industry-standard multibutton computer mice as "inelegant." He had removed on/off power buttons on desktop units. He had removed buttons from elevators in multilevel Apple retail stores, along with standard retail queues and counters. Rarely if ever could he be seen wearing a shirt with buttons.

But for the iPhone, Mr. Jobs had removed the one physical feature that *every* phone in the world shared: the keypad. In fact, there was no thumbwheel, no stylus, no buttons to punch, dial, click, or scroll, except a single home button. Even by Apple design standards, long known to honor clean and aesthetically pleasing lines, the iPhone had the sparest design ever conceived. With a flick of a finger across a device the surface of which was almost entirely touchscreen, you could access vivid, three-dimensional displays of music, photos, contacts, and movies. The keyboard was soft-wired, and virtual.

And what followed was a study in seduction. The conventional thinkers weighed in immediately, much as they did after *The Sopranos* finale. Detractors criticized the lack of a keyboard, as well as Apple's choice to select a single service provider, AT&T. They criticized AT&T's slower network, and minimized the ability of the iPhone to switch to faster Wi-Fi networks. And then two things happened almost simultaneously.

First, the attacks served only to embolden the vast number of Apple loyalists, giving them something to react to and defend. The blogosphere was fully ignited. Support became exponentially greater every day. Second, Steve Jobs swatted aside the critics' concerns. When the *Wall Street Journal*'s technology columnist Walt Mossberg asked Jobs to defend his decision to omit a physical keyboard, Jobs responded: "The iPhone's keyboard lets us use far more sophisticated software to improve accuracy, customize the keyboard for specific applications, and of course remove the keyboard when it's not needed, freeing iPhone's entire large screen for reading email, browsing the Web, looking at maps, enjoying photos and movies, and doing things we haven't yet invented. We think the iPhone's keyboard is one of its greatest assets and competitive advantages."

The very notion of an iPhone in any shape or form sprang from Jobs's hatred of his previous cell phone, and every cell phone prior to the iPhone. They were far too difficult to use, one of the most frustrating features being the tiny keyboards.

It wasn't long before the iPhone was hailed as one of the most-hyped products ever to hit the market. Which, ironically, it wasn't. To hype something means to *push* it heavily through the use of various marketing, sales, and media tactics. But that's exactly the opposite of what Apple did. In fact, they actually *stopped* doing a good number of things.

Along with the missing buttons came an apparently missing marketing campaign. There was no multi-month promotion, no multichannel publicity, and no multimillion-dollar advertising. Steve Jobs's MacWorld demonstration was essentially it. His spare design was coupled with an equally spare marketing strategy: announce once and *do nothing.* No clever commercials until just days before the on-sale date. No calculated information leaks to entice the media. No appearances by the charismatic Jobs on television. No sweeping demo model program for the influential technology journalists. No advance reviews in print or online media. No evangelistic outreach to the Apple cult. No special introductory offer or handset rebate—the entry-level price tag was triple the average price for a new phone. No preordering. In fact, Apple limited distribution to in-store sales only, and all stores were to begin in synchronized fashion at the predetermined time of 6 p.m. the evening of June 29, 2007. It was a most elegantly executed "stop doing" strategy.

When *Fortune* magazine in March 2008 named Apple "America's Most Admired Company" as well as "Most Admired for Innovation," honors owing largely to the success of the iPhone, Jobs revealed that a stop-doing strategy figured centrally into Apple's approach: "We tend to focus much more. People think focus means saying yes to the thing you've got to focus on. But that's not what it means at all. It means saying no to the hundred other good ideas that there are. You have to pick carefully. I'm actually as proud of many of the things we haven't done as the things we have done."

By the time the iPhone finally went on sale, well over half the U.S. and British mobile phone market was aware of it, and nearly twenty million Americans had expressed interest in buying one, regardless of the price or potential wait. The iPhone "tipped" well before it even hit the market.

The iPhone phenomenon exemplified the seductive mystique of the *non finito* in a business setting. But to better understand the allure of the unknown, the unexplained, and the incomplete, you have to understand a bit about both human nature and how the brain works.

*c.*

When the Greek philosopher Aristotle maintained that "All men by nature desire to know," he was referring to human curiosity, or as Samuel Johnson called it: "the first passion and last." To be curious is to seek what is different, what stands apart, and what doesn't make immediate sense, without regard for whether or not the findings are even good for us. Tell someone *not* to do something, and it creates an instant temptation: think of Eve eating the apple, Pandora opening the box, and of course the infamous cat killed by curiosity. Sit just within earshot of the couple at the next table passionately whispering something that might have to do with last night's escapades and we find ourselves straining to hear all the juicy details, to the point of putting our own conversation on hold.

Curiosity—aka the need to know—is part of what's behind the impact of not just the iPhone strategy, but also of elegance and the missing piece in general. But we don't need philosophers to tell us we're by nature curious. We know that. What we may not know is why.

In his seminal 1890 work *The Principles of Psychology*, William James detailed two different kinds of curiosity. The first is an *emotional* response to something, and instinctive. Anytime you see something new, out of the ordinary, or unusual to you, your attention is aroused, which triggers a desire to explore and make sense out of the situation. Most higher-order animals exhibit exploratory behavior when faced with something unfamiliar or unexpected. Dogs aren't just admiring each other's scent when they meet for the first time and perform the obligatory sniff tests, they're attempting to construct a thorough canine history. The second type of curiosity, "scientific curiosity," James described as the brain's response "to an inconsistency or a gap in its knowledge, just as the musical brain responds to discord in what it hears." Nearly all of the psychological research into curiosity over the past century derives from William James's work.

In the late 1950s, University of Toronto psychologist Daniel Berlyne expanded upon James's work by looking at curiosity-seeking behavior along a more voluntary dimension, dividing curiosity into two major categories, *diversive* and *specific*. Berlyne defined diversive curiosity as the human tendency to seek out novelty, take risks, and search for adventure. Specific curiosity, on the other hand, is the natural inclination to investigate something in order to understand it. Berlyne determined four primary external stimuli that arouse curiosity: complexity, novelty, uncertainty, and conflict (defined as the violation of expectations). He also discovered that there's a specific trigger point for curiosity: if the level of stimulation is too low, there's no real motivation to explore; if it's too high, the result is anxiety and avoidance. In other words, in order for something to motivate us to act on our curiosity, it needs to hit a kind of "sweet spot" for one or more of the four stimuli.

The late musicologist Leonard Meyer came to a similar conclusion in his 1956 book *Emotion and Meaning in Music*.

Meyer used Ludwig van Beethoven's technique of establishing and building toward a harmonic pattern but then denying the listener that pattern in full until the end of the piece to illustrate how music stimulates the mind by creating tension. Meyer showed through an extensive analysis of fifty bars in Beethoven's String Quartet no. 14 in C-Sharp Minor that the composer was deliberately flirting with the listener, using one incomplete variation after another to suggest the pattern and delaying full resolution until the final chord was played. Meyer suggested that the value of a musical work was directly correlated to how well its level of complexity engaged the listener. Works in which no expectations were met were ultimately unsatisfying, as were those in which the audience's every expectation was met. Meyer concluded that "as soon as the unexpected, or for that matter the surprising, is experienced . . . the mind may suspend judgment, trusting that what follows will clarify the meaning of the unexpected consequent. If no clarification takes place, the mind may reject the whole stimulus and irritation will set in."

Forty years later George Loewenstein of Carnegie Mellon University reinterpreted the psychological work on curiosity from William James forward in a sweeping review, and synthesized his own derivation, calling it the "information-gap theory." After exploring all of the theoretical forms and types of curiosity-seeking, Loewenstein was able to confirm William James's knowledge gap—when we perceive there to be a gap in our knowledge, we feel deprived, a feeling we label as curiosity. And it's our desire to alleviate that feeling that motivates us to obtain the missing information. How deeply deprived we feel is relative to how we perceive the gap. It all depends on how much we know and how much we want to know.

For example, I know that there are countless other people in the world far more knowledgeable than I on a great many topics. I don't feel deprived in any way, essentially because the gap is so wide and so nebulous that I could never hope to fathom it, much less close it. I only feel deprived when I'm aware of a specific individual who happens to be more knowledgeable than I am in *my* particular field of interest. Especially when he or she is at the same dinner party and proceeds to point out the gap at every opportunity. I become more curious about the missing information that will enable me to close that particular gap, and even go beyond, so that the next time we attend the same function, I can help that person feel likewise deprived.

Loewenstein labeled this phenomenon a "situational determinate" of curiosity, a finding that held several important implications. First, the intensity of our curiosity about a particular missing piece of information is dependent on how well we think it will close the gap we're most interested in. Second, we are more likely to be more curious about a single piece of missing information when we think it will help us solve the problem all at once, as opposed to getting us incrementally closer to the solution. Third, curiosity increases with perceived knowledge, meaning the more we know, the more we want to know. Loewenstein tested his ideas in several important studies.

In one study, participants were shown a grid of forty-five squares on a computer screen. A picture was hidden behind the grid, and using the mouse to click on a square would reveal a small part of the entire image. Loewenstein used two different pictures: one of a group of animals, one of a solitary animal. Unaware that their curiosity was being studied, participants were told that the grid was simply a practice screen to get familiar with the computer mouse, and to click on at least five of the squares to get the hang of it. Curiosity was to be measured by how many squares over and above the required five got exposed. There was a cost to gaining information—a four-second delay between click and reveal—so participants really had to be interested in seeing the bigger picture in order to keep clicking. Sure enough, the people clicking on the single animal picture, whose complete identity was harder to determine by a few clicks than was the group of animals, exposed a significantly larger number of squares.

In another study, Loewenstein showed people from zero to three photographs, one by one, of different male or female body parts. The body parts consisted of torso, hands, and feet. He then asked each participant how curious they were to see the picture of the whole person, giving them a choice between getting a small monetary bonus of under a dollar or seeing the whole photograph. The more parts someone had seen, the more curious they were to see the whole person.

From these and other experiments, and from the work that had come before, Loewenstein predicted that curiosity will arise spontaneously when certain situational factors alert us that some information is missing: "The posing of a question or presentation of a riddle or puzzle confronts the individual directly with missing information and is therefore perhaps the most straightforward curiosity inducer. Exposure to a sequence of events with an anticipated but unknown resolution will almost inevitably create curiosity to know the outcome. The violation of expectations often triggers a search for explanation, and curiosity is frequently a major factor motivating the search. Possession of information by someone else also causes curiosity."

But there's a slight catch. The theory rests on the assumption of awareness *and* appreciation of the gap between what we already know and what we want to know in the first place. Not only do we need to perceive the gap, but the missing information—the idea itself—needs to be unique; it can't be a shoulder-shrug when it eventually gets discovered. Loewenstein himself declared that "a failure to appreciate what one does not know would constitute an absolute barrier to curiosity. There is good reason to believe that such barriers are pervasive."

In the late 1990s, a few years after Loewenstein published his review, marketing scientists Dilip Soman and Satya Menon grappled with that very assumption, seeking to answer the question of how to get people to click on an online ad.

Soman and Menon wanted to explore two crucial issues in business management: first, how advertisers of new products and services can overcome the difficulty of motivating people to learn about radically new and thus unfamiliar features and benefits, and second, how Internet advertisers can motivate Web shoppers to actively acquire product information. The pair hoped their studies would demonstrate that the power of curiosity can be harnessed in specific ways to design an effective advertising strategy that engages people in the search for information about a new product. What they discovered was revealing.

Soman and Menon ran two experiments in 1997 that centered on a fictitious product, a digital camera called the Sony QV. (At that time, digital cameras were new to the market and not nearly the standard they are today.) Soman and Menon created two sets of ads for the Sony QV, each of which focused on one of the two primary benefits of the camera: its ability to create digital images that could be manipulated electronically and its capacity to send those images through e-mail in unique ways. One or the other of these two benefits became the curiosity trigger and was displayed prominently in the headline of the ad. For each trigger, Soman and Menon designed three ads with the same headline and visual treatment but with different-sized knowledge gaps: narrow, medium, and wide. The narrow gap ad clearly revealed that the Sony QV was a digital camera and gave details on many of the features. The medium gap ad provided a clue that the Sony QV was a camera, but withheld any further details. The wide gap ad gave no clues or information whatsoever beyond the QV being a new Sony product.

In the first test, volunteers were randomly assigned to view one of the six different versions of the Sony QV ad, designed in a traditional print medium. Each person completed a four-question survey constructed to measure their curiosity: How curious do you feel about this product? How interested would you be in reading more about this product? How involved did you feel in reading the advertisement about the product? How interested would you be in checking out this product at a store?

The results were surprising. Whatever the trigger benefit being used, those viewing the medium gap ads were twice as curious about the Sony QV than those viewing either the narrow or the wide gap ads. In fact, only the medium gap ad created the perception that the Sony QV was a highly novel product.

Soman and Menon went online for the second test, which used the same basic structure. This time, though, subjects were randomly assigned to view two different versions of a cyber magazine consisting of eight pages of articles interspersed with four ads, one of which was the Sony QV test ad. The first version included one of the six ads covering the different knowledge gaps. The second issue carried full information about the Sony QV. All the ads in both versions had clickable buttons that linked to other Web sites that provided more information. In other words, to find out more about the Sony QV in the first version, you had to click through to another site that contained more information. In the second version, even though the ad gave full information, you could still click through to find out more. In both cases, a product frequently asked questions (FAQ) link was provided, which led to a page that was "Under Construction" but prompted the clicker to submit a question they wanted answered after viewing the Sony QV ad.

In addition to the same four-question survey collected in the first experiment, Soman and Menon measured the click-through volume and the number of questions submitted. What they found was a fairly dramatic inverted-U-shaped relationship between the level of information provided and the degree of interest generated. The medium gap ad was far more effective in motivating search behavior. The total time spent on the information search and the survey was significantly higher, which suggested that the biggest impact of curiosity might not just be the quantity of time spent, but the quality of attention paid.

Soman and Menon concluded that the best way to stimulate interest is to do three things, consistent with Loewenstein's theory. The first is to arouse curiosity by demonstrating a moderate gap in the observer's knowledge. Second, provide just enough information to make them want to resolve their curiosity. Third, give them time to try to resolve their curiosity on their own.

It's a pretty good seduction strategy. If you think about it for a moment, it boils down to playing hard to get. Evidence of its effectiveness is present in the examples discussed previously in this chapter. But while all this behavioral research is invaluable, with important implications for everyone with an idea, my own curiosity was piqued by the question of what underlying physiology might be responsible for the observed behavior. I wanted to know more of what was actually behind the Soman and Menon strategy. To answer that question, I talked to someone whose work and life revolve around the inner workings of the mind and the brain: neuroscientist Dr. Jeffrey Schwartz, of UCLA's Neuroscience Institute, co-author of *The Mind and the Brain* and one of the world's foremost authorities on the subject.

*d.*

The private practice office of Dr. Jeffrey Schwartz is located away from the UCLA campus and the rigors of clinical research, on the cusp of Santa Monica. One's first impression of Schwartz is that he surely must have a million ideas running through his mind at any given moment; somehow he manages to express a good many of them through a surprisingly animated discourse in a highly compressed time frame. He's one of the few individuals in his field who blends philosophy, and even religion, with science. I'll discuss him more in the last chapter of the book, but for the moment I'm most interested in why gaps—the ambiguous, uncertain *nothingness* of a compelling idea—are so seductive.

What Jeff Schwartz will tell you is that the human brain is a pattern-making, pattern-recognizing, pattern-*locking* machine. All day long, unbeknownst to us, and for the most part uncontrolled by us, our brains work to basically TiVo every single experience, sending sensory information in the form of electrical impulses into our cerebral cortex, the so-called gray matter that houses the brain's higher functions. Jeff told me that every new experience is automatically stored as data in our brain. The process is additive and cumulative, and generally goes unedited. Even though the electrical impulses themselves disappear in milliseconds, their passage to the nerve cells triggers a grouping mechanism, filing new information with other like data as it comes in, which in turn creates specific and unique patterns. Different patterns combine to make memories and perceptions. Those connections are reinforced over time and quickly become mental models— mind-sets, biases, and paradigms. Those mental models allow us to function, for the most part, much more efficiently and effectively, by helping us rapidly sift data and sort information into useful knowledge, according to whether it confirms or contradicts the strong patterns already embedded in our minds. (On later visits, I would come to learn more about the rather potent downside to these patterns, as I'll describe in the final chapter.)

As I discovered from Jeff Schwartz, our obliviousness to the patterns in our brain is what makes observational comedy so funny. The best comedies and comedians are those able to invoke what Schwartz refers to as the Impartial Spectator, a term coined by Adam Smith in his 1759 treatise *The Theory of Moral Sentiments.* Smith defined the Impartial Spectator as the ability to stand outside of yourself and watch yourself in action. Modern comedy points out the universal patterns of behavior and mental models we all share. What we're really laughing at when we watch shows like *Seinfeld, Curb Your*

*Enthusiasm*, and *The Office* is the recognition of the patterns in our own behavior, almost as if we're outside of ourselves, watching in amusement.

How does all this relate to curiosity? Our mind, like nature, detests a vacuum. When a pattern is broken in a dramatic way, we take notice. When something is suddenly different, and in particular missing, two things happen. First, we are taken by surprise. When the television screens of the viewers watching the last episode of *The Sopranos* abruptly went black, the first reaction was one of simple shock. The mental model of how a television episode is supposed to end was shattered. When the audience at MacWorld viewed the iPhone for the first time, they were completely caught off guard. The mental model of what a phone, "smart" or otherwise, is supposed to look like was turned upside down. In both cases, the first reaction was indignation at the pattern change. But shortly thereafter, in both cases, the element of surprise is what ignited curiosity, the direct result of the "violation of expectations" that Berlyne and Loewenstein identified as a key situational determinant of curiosity. And in both cases, Soman and Menon's first recommendation to demonstrate a gap in knowledge held true.

The second thing that happens is that we seek to fill in the gap and connect the dots to resolve our curiosity. This explains what happened following the final episode of *The Sopranos*. It explains the mysterious "pull" of Apple's nonexistent marketing thrust. In each case, and in accordance with Soman and Menon's second principle, just enough information was given to tantalize viewers and future iPhone buyers into resolving their curiosity.

As it turns out, we are hardwired to fill in the gaps and to make sense of what we see. At the beginning of the twentieth century, the Gestalt movement in psychology, which focused on this aspect of perception, was in high gear. The term *Gestalt* was coined by Austrian psychologist Christian von Ehrenfels, who published *On Gestalt Qualities* in 1890, the same year William James published *The Principles of Psychology.* Gestalt essentially refers to how we tend to see related parts as a unified whole, rather than a simple sum of the parts. A fundamental principle of Gestalt perception is that of closure. Take a look at the images below. Most people will see a circle, a square, and a triangle.

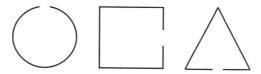

Note that in reality, there is no circle, square, or triangle. Ths cn b hrd fr ppl to cmprhnd; howvr, mst ppl cn ndrstntd ths sntnc wth lttl prblm. Our brains do a lot of filling in for us. There is no sophisticated term for this phenomenon, either, other than simply "filling in." It's guesswork, really, by the brain. Neuroscientists love to demonstrate just how smart this guesswork is by demonstrating the effect of the physiological blind spot of the eye, which is called the *punctum caecum* in medical literature. You likely have seen or done this before, but in case you haven't, here's how it works.

Hold the book up close to your face. Cover your right eye and focus your left eye on the X. Now slowly, *really* slowly, move the book away from you. At some point the O will disappear and in its place will be not a hole, but a uniform gray background, courtesy of the "filling in" power of your brain. It works on both eyes, so if you want the X to disappear, just do the exact reverse.

What happened? The O disappears the moment the image falls on a small patch of retina called the optic disc, an area that is devoid of receptors. The optic disc is the place where the optic nerve pierces the retina as it exits the eyeball and heads back toward your brain. Using what's called a "surface interpolation" process, your brain fills in the spot with information taken from the immediate area, in this case the gray background. Neuroscientists believe this ability evolved as a survival mechanism: by computing and rendering representations of continuous surfaces and contours, early humans could "see" an entire predator half-obscured by trees or tall grass. When you see your boss peeking in at you through the Venetian blinds in your office, you see your whole boss, not a sliced-up boss, which is probably a good thing. Back in the Victorian days, physicist Sir David Brewster attributed the filling-in perception to God, whom he called the "Divine Artificer."

Interestingly, the blind spot can be pretty big, almost the size of ten full moons in the night sky. If you get bored with the exercise above, which I hope you do fairly quickly, you can always close or cover one eye and look around the room with the other. It shouldn't take too long to get good at aiming your blind spot at any small object to make it disappear. King Charles II of England used to aim his blind spot at a prisoner's head in order to visually decapitate him just before the actual beheading. This technique can come in handy, such as when the pesky know-it-all is regaling the group at that dinner party mentioned earlier.

Your eyes trick you with the help of your brain in other ways. Hold three fingers up close to your face, and spread them as wide as you can. Keeping your eyes unfocused, slowly move your hand away from your face. Stop when the three fingers become four. This time, your brain actually went beyond its filling-in to downright deceptive fabrication. Now, you may claim my instructing you to cross your eyes or keep them unfocused is dirty pool, so take a look at the illustration below, without doing anything. Do you "see" the phantom dots in the gaps? That would be your brain doing its filling in again, and you can now officially declare that you are seeing things.

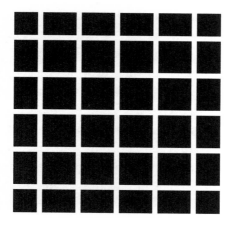

There are a number of studies which show that, and pardon the Yogi Berra–ism, it's not just your eyes that are blind, but your ears as well. A 1970 *Scientific American* article by psychologist Richard Warren at the University of Wisconsin described how, when presented with sentences in which portions had been deleted and replaced by a noise such as a cough, people heard the sentences as if they were intact. When Warren preceded the syllable *eel* with a cough in the sentence "It was found that the *[cough]*eel was on the axle," people heard the word *wheel.* When he replaced the last word with *table,* they heard *meal.* When the last word was *orange,* they heard *peel.* A decade later, psychologist Takayuki Sasaki in Japan discovered that the exact same effect could be observed when certain notes of a familiar song melody were deleted and replaced with a loud sound burst. Listeners heard the missing tones appear through the noise. Musical composers, particularly in the field of classical and romantic guitar, have long exploited the blind ear.

The point here is that a good part of your brain's creativity—remember, it's making this stuff up on its own, stuff that just plain doesn't exist—is tied to the patterning ability Jeff Schwartz explained to me. Patterns help provide a strong context, which in turn provides meaning and sense, things that most of us crave. Context-creating patterns are something we discovered in our short spin through Symmetryville, and it is this patterning ability that has everything to do with how fully our imagination engages when we're presented with knowledge gaps. But what about the other two parts to the Soman and Menon strategy?

*e.*

As Soman and Menon demonstrated, there is a curiosity trigger point linked to the breadth of the knowledge gap. This second part of the strategy, though—the need for just the right amount and type of clues—is perhaps more art than science. Artists like Leonardo da Vinci with his *sfumato*, and Michelangelo and Cézanne with their *non finito*, were able to strike the proper balance in an intuitive way, perhaps because they were masters in the field of visual perception.

Take a look at the figures below. As your eyes move left to right, note how your attention and interest shift with the size of the colored space. At the image on the left, our attention is focused on the small black space. The middle image appeals to us; thanks to its bilateral symmetry, our attention is balanced. At the far right image, we see essentially the same image as the one on the far left, only because of the color shift, we now see a gap to be filled in. When looking for the trigger point, it helps to remember that *we essentially ignore the majority of what's there and focus on what isn't.*

Think of the inverted U-shape Soman and Menon discovered in their research. To achieve a high level of curiosity, you'd want to be as close to the apex as possible, meaning you'd want to avoid giving too little or too much information. It's hard to know exactly where the midrange is, but usually the error is made on the "too much information" side. For example, in a 2008 study conducted at the University of Iowa, researchers found that people like a product less when they know too much about it. In one test, volunteers were given the opportunity to pick a video to watch. They were told one of the movies had received nothing but rave reviews from critics, while the other had received mixed reviews. Those selecting the movie with mixed reviews were more optimistic about their choice than those picking the movie with uniformly positive reviews. In a second test, volunteers were asked what they thought of a hand lotion. In a third test, they were asked for their opinion of chocolate. In each of these last two cases, one group was given lots of information, the other group far less. In both tests, the group that was given detailed product information was much less optimistic than the one given just a little bit of information. The study's authors labeled this the "Blissful Ignorance Effect."

Perhaps the makers of the U.K. candy favorite Cadbury Dairy Milk received a preliminary report on the chocolate test. In August 2007, Cadbury Schweppes's ad agency, Fallon Worldwide, aired a ninety-second television commercial for the chocolate bars, featuring a gorilla, or rather, a man in a movie-quality gorilla suit, seated at a drum set in a recording studio while Phil Collins's "In the Air Tonight" plays. For the first full minute, we see only close-ups of the motionless gorilla, who looks to be contemplating the music and preparing for the performance of a lifetime. The next twenty-six seconds shows the gorilla rocking out on the drums as if his life depended on it. The only reference to the product was a four-second shot of the chocolate bar at the very end of the spot, the tagline being "A glass and a half full of joy." Not only did sales rise 10 percent in the two months following the ad, but by December the ad had been viewed over seven million times on YouTube.

The third plank of the Soman and Menon seduction

strategy—that of giving people time to resolve their curiosity—is perhaps the trickiest task, but also the most interesting and most seductive. It's why Sudoku is so addicting, and why detective stories from Sherlock Holmes to the television show *CSI* are so popular. Jeff Schwartz confirmed for me that resolving our curiosity, whether receiving the surprise *aha!* at the end of a great whodunnit or filling in the final Sudoku box, activates the satisfaction center in the brain, which fMRI scans show is triggered by external stimuli associated with reward. That structure, called the striatum, is connected to the frontal lobe, which directs logical thought and action toward the achievement of a goal. That connection delivers pleasure by releasing dopamine, a neurochemical transmitter linked to our mental and physical health, as well as to addictive behavior. In other words, "filling in" is hedonically satisfying, and delivers a feel-good rush that makes you immediately crave more. (I'm fairly certain that this is what's responsible for the daily desire of some to visit a mall and fill up shopping bags.)

The more interesting element is timing, which, as the cliché goes, is everything. Although the gaps were much different in length, both David Chase and Steve Jobs demonstrated expert timing: Chase in his post-finale announcement that all the clues needed to arrive at a story conclusion were present in the episode, and Jobs in giving six months between his pre-launch announcement of the iPhone and the on-sale date.

But here again, the brain has its way with you on these timing issues, and curiosity often trumps regret. You swore that you'd never again help a friend move after the last time, when your back was sore for three weeks. Now your best friend calls to tell you he and his wife have just bought the perfect house in an amazing location at an incredible price, something you simply must see to believe. Escrow closes the week after next. Oh . . . and can you help them move? "Sure, I'd love to. Can't wait to see it." This despite your past experience, despite your knowing better. Why do you accept? Because the temporal gap is just right, and your brain's filling-in mechanism has determined that a couple of weeks is an okay period to wait for your curiosity to be resolved. Had he asked you to help them move today, you would have declined, the unpleasantness of your past moving experience being vivid enough in your mind to help you make an iron-clad case for why putting up rabbit fencing around the tomatoes couldn't possibly wait another day. Had he asked you to help three months from now, way too wide a temporal gap, your likely response would have been something along the lines of "Call me as it gets closer." But with two weeks, the timing was right and the lure of curiosity resolved—the chance to see the "perfect" house—trumps potential regret.

In 2005 Dutch psychologists Eric van Dijk and Marcel Zeelenberg furthered our knowledge about the link between curiosity and regret in uncertain situations by exploring an interesting question: What happens when a decision that protects you from regret simultaneously prevents you from resolving your curiosity? Basically, Dijk and Zeelenberg were looking for the fatal flaw in the information-gap theory. But what they found confirmed its viability. Volunteers were told they could choose to receive either fifteen euros or a small sealed package after completing a series of questions for a scientific study. In other words, the choice pitted the ability to avoid regret by taking the guaranteed fifteen euros against unresolved curiosity, namely marching through life without closure on the question: What was in that package? When they were given a hint that what was in the package was round, exactly twice as many people chose the package over the safer choice of fifteen euros. Curiosity trumped regret. The interplay between the two is part of what made the game show *Let's Make a Deal* so popular. But what happens when curiosity never gets resolved?

In 1989, the Infiniti luxury division of Nissan Motor Corporation demonstrated clearly what happens when only the first two of the three tactics in the Soman and Menon strategy are executed. To introduce consumers to the new brand, Infiniti launched a series of print and television commercials. Meant to arouse curiosity and drive people to showrooms, the ads never showed the Infiniti cars. Instead, readers and viewers saw serene images such as a pebble dropping into water or a lone tree surrounded by mist, meant to suggest that driving an Infiniti produced a Zen-like connection between man and nature. The ads indeed created initial curiosity and intrigue. But there was no way to resolve that curiosity, ever. Months after the launch, the cars themselves still had never been shown. Dealers and consumers became critical. The intriguing mystery of "what's the car look like?" soon became "who cares about the car?" The Infiniti campaign fizzled, came to be known as "rocks and trees," and eventually became a joke. Comedian Jay Leno quipped, "Infiniti may not be doing so well, but, hey, at least sales of rocks and trees are skyrocketing."

There is one final story to tell, a personal account of a rather popular and highly entertaining application of the seductive *non finito* idea.

### *f.*

The *New Yorker* magazine's cartoons are arguably the world's funniest. Many subscribers will admit to the fact that, like me, they read all of the cartoons first whenever they pick up their new issue. Each cartoon is a single, spare panel, and the humor can be obscure at times. I recall an episode of *Seinfeld* called "The Cartoon," in which Elaine marches to the *New Yorker* offices demanding a sketch be explained to her, only to hear that "Cartoons are like gossamer, and one doesn't dissect gossamer."

On April 25, 2005, the *New Yorker* magazine's cartoon editor Robert Mankoff announced that the annual cartoon caption contest that had begun in 1998 would become a weekly event.

The cartoon caption contest is simple in concept: a staff artist draws a complete panel, but with an obviously missing piece, the caption, which the contestant must supply using twenty-five words or less. The contest is deeply entrenched in popular American culture, so much so that it's been the topic of several academic studies. One study conducted in 2006 by the University of Michigan looked into how winners arrived at their idea, discovering that the vast majority came up with their ideas in a flash of insight. That prompted a second study in which volunteer winners were asked to write a caption on the spot, to see what happens to humor when you make someone anxious. Conclusive results aren't available as of this writing, but an educated guess might be that it turns into aggravated assault.

Following the announcement Mankoff was asked in an interview what the original intent behind the contest was, to which he replied: "What we were trying to do, mainly, was to create this odd sort of challenge for readers and discover whether the results were interesting. In other words, we wanted to know how inspiration was sparked when someone was looking at an image with an incongruity in it that called out for a comic line."

The *New Yorker* contest is as blatantly a modern-day version of ongoing *non finito* as you can get. And seductive? Mankoff says they receive between 6,000 and 12,000 entries each week. Here's how it works. Each Monday, a new contest is announced on the back page of the magazine. The contest closes at midnight the following Sunday, so you have one week to submit your entry on the *New Yorker* Web site. Once the contest closes, the entries are reviewed and categorized by the cartoon staff, who pick three finalists, announced the week after the close of the contest. Readers then vote on their favorite of the three. The contest actually follows the Soman and Menon strategy very well.

On February 24, 2008, I submitted my caption entry for the panel shown below, drawn by cartoonist Jack Ziegler, of a couple wearing hazardous material suits in a bed.

It was my third attempt in as many years. On the previous two occasions I had entered on a whim, and just for fun, not really hoping to win, not really putting much creative thought into it. This time, I had a purpose in mind: to engage my imagination fully in the *non finito* experience. Using some of the concepts I'll discuss in the last two chapters, I gave it my best shot. Four days later *New Yorker* staff artist Farley Katz called me to let me know I was a finalist. On March 17, 2008, I won the contest. The full cartoon ap-

"Next time can we just get flu shots like everyone else?"
©*The New Yorker Magazine, 2008. Artwork by Jack Ziegler. Caption provided by Matthew E. May. All Rights Reserved.*

peared in the March 24 issue, and I received a completed panel signed by Mr. Ziegler. Most important, I gained the ability to share my own *non finito* story with you.

As the discoveries we've explored on this part of the search point out, the seductive aspect of elegance requires the presence of absence. But it is not just that a piece is missing. The trick is knowing just which piece to *make* missing.

# CHAPTER FOUR

# Laws of Subtraction

WHEN ASKED HOW he sculpted his famous statue of David, the marble masterpiece considered to be the image of the perfect man, Michelangelo replied, "I saw David through the stone, and I simply chipped away everything that was not David." Aviator Antoine de Saint-Exupéry, author of *The Little Prince*, picked up on Michelangelo's implication when he observed that "perfection is achieved not when there is nothing more to add, but when there is nothing left to take away." Novelist Italo Calvino wrote that "My working method has more often than not involved the subtraction of weight. Above all I have tried to remove weight from the structure of stories and language."

The laws under which elegance can be achieved—those governing the use of symmetry and seduction—are subtractive. But if, as we have discovered, we are by nature prone to fill in—to add—by what means can we reconcile and exploit this seeming paradox? What are the most effective ways to fight the enemy of elegance, which is not complexity, but excess?

*a.*

There is nothing really "in and out" about In-N-Out Burger. The lines are always long, but it's well worth the wait. In-N-Out Burger is a Southern California institution with a cult-like following not unlike that of Apple or Starbucks. Its reputation extends far beyond the West Coast, though, and indulging in a Double-Double—two 100% beef patties plus two slices of American cheese, hand-leafed lettuce, bread spread, tomato, with or without onions, on a fresh-baked bun—is on the to-do list of many tourists. The company has in the last few years pushed beyond California to neighboring Nevada and Arizona, and when one opened in Scottsdale, the wait was four hours. Even people who shun fast food seem to love In-N-Out. In fact, it is one of only a couple establishments favored by Eric Schlosser in his book *Fast Food Nation,* an indictment of American fast food.

In-N-Out Burger was founded by Harry and Esther Snyder in 1948 in the Los Angeles suburb of Baldwin Park. It was Harry's innovation to start a drive-through burger stand where customers could order through a two-way speaker box. Back then, carhops and big canopied burger joints were the norm. The company has remained family-owned and privately run since its inception—so private its executives rarely speak to the media—even though Harry, Esther, and oldest son Guy, each of whom took turns at the helm, have passed away. Based on the Snyders' standing philosophy, every new manager learns at the In-N-Out University to "Give customers the freshest, highest quality foods you can buy and provide them with friendly service in a sparkling clean environment." In-N-Out Burger is known for its consistent quality, freshness—you can watch the potatoes as they are hand-cut daily for the fries, shakes are made from real ice cream, and there are no freezers or microwaves—and simple menu. But most important, In-N-Out Burger understands the power of the missing piece.

To begin with, the menu has only four food items. You can order a Hamburger, a Cheeseburger, a Double-Double, and French Fries. The fifth item is a beverage. You can partake in the standard array of Coca-Cola products, or order one of three flavors of milkshake: chocolate, vanilla, or strawberry. *That's it.* Or is it?

One reason for the cultish phenomenon of the company is the "secret menu." You have to be in the know to be privy to it. The most interesting thing about the secret menu is that not only do the items on it far outnumber those on the published menu, but they are completely unique concoctions, dreamed up by customers, universally prepared according to a cross-company formula, and well beyond Starbucks' approach of allowing tweaks to an already extensive menu. When you order, say, a "tall, extra-hot, nonfat, double-shot, four-pump, no-whip mocha" at Starbucks, your receipt simply reads "TL MOCHA." When you order a "2x4" or a "3-by-Meat" or a "Flying Dutchman" at any In-N-Out Burger, it will appear on the receipt just as you ordered it. But nowhere will you see anything even remotely referring to it on the menu posted above the register.

There are about a dozen "standard" off-menu items. A 2x4 is a burger with two beef patties and four slices of cheese. You can order any combination of meat-X-cheese you desire: 3x3, 4x4, etc. In fact, Wikipedia shows a photograph of a 20x20, and on a Halloween weekend in October 2004, Zappos.com CEO Tony Hsieh and blogger What Up Willy ordered and ate—with a team of six others—a 100x100, consuming nearly 20,000 calories in less than two hours. This, of course, is an extreme case of "filling in" and "filling up," and should not be tried at home.

A 3-by-Meat is sans cheese, and again, you can order any number-by-meat. The Animal Style is a mustard-cooked patty, with pickles, extra sauce, and grilled onions. Protein Style is for those watching their carbs: no bun; instead, the makings are wrapped in a big leaf of iceberg lettuce. (This is actually quite good, and a favorite of the women in my family.) A Grilled Cheese is a cheeseburger without the burger, and great if you're not a fan of red meat, while the Veggie Burger is actually a bun with whole grilled onions, sauce, lettuce, and double tomato. The Flying Dutchman is simply two patties and two slices of cheese—no bun, no nothing else—on a paper plate. The Extra Toast is literally that: the bun's left on the grill longer for crispiness. That's just the burgers. Fries can be Animal Style, topped with sauce, onions, and cheese, Light or Well-Done, which are undercooked or overcooked, respectively. Shakes can be ordered regular, or Swirl or Neopolitan, meaning two or three of the flavors mixed.

In-N-Out has never changed their menu to reflect these items. In other words, it creates a sense of mystique around what is missing from the menu. The customers do the filling in, In-N-Out does the filling up. By resisting formal menu expansion they've avoided the self-defeating overkill seen in consumer electronics, with its "feature creep," and the resulting "feature fatigue." They understand our desire to fill in, and they simply go with it, keeping their wares pared back but enabling their patrons to add their own personal touch.

They don't actively promote, or even pay much attention to, the secret menu. In fact, when you talk to the executives at In-N-Out, they seem as mystified as customers by the presence of the secret menu, but they do understand the completely intangible value of the tailored touch. Their only rule is "to do whatever the customer wants done to a burger." Most important, they understand that to expand the formal menu could only detract from an important reason why In-N-Out is so very popular and successful. They understand that there is nothing elegant about excess.

*b.*

Elite sports training demands stressing muscles with steadily increasing loads, a technique widely known as progressive resistance. In fact, it demands overloading the muscles, in the sense that conventional methods work muscles to fatigue and failure in order to activate a healing process that strengthens and grows muscle fiber. But increasing the load requires increased recovery time in order to avoid overtraining. There comes a point where longer and tougher workouts simply don't work. Returns diminish and performance can actually recede. At that point, an elite athlete's peak level becomes unsustainable and inconsistency plagues performance.

That's exactly what happened to champion cyclist Lance Armstrong. Going into the 2004 season, Armstrong had the opportunity to make history by becoming the first rider ever to win six Tour de France titles, and to do so in consecutive years, having the year before matched Spaniard Miguel Indurain's record of five straight wins in the early 1990s. But

Armstrong had struggled in his 2003 effort, winning the coveted *maillot jaune*—the yellow jersey that is the crown jewel of professional cycling—by just over a minute. Going into the 2004 season, he faced an overload challenge. The problem was that he had run out of hours in the day to train, improvement had stalled, and too much energy had been spent during the early spring months shedding the previous winter's weight gain. Like every other pro cyclist, Lance slacked off during the winter and allowed himself to pack on a few pounds—the nemesis of anyone trying to climb a mountain on a bike. That meant focusing on weight loss for the first few months, restricting food intake, weighing food—a certain diet obsession that not only made life more unpleasant, but detracted from the very energy required to complete a six-hour training ride.

Armstrong knew from the previous year that his usual training regimen wouldn't work anymore. The field was too young, hungry, and competitive, while he was fast approaching the twilight of a magnificent cycling career. He had attained star status, written bestselling books on his death-defying journey back from testicular cancer, and was fast becoming a global lightning rod in the fight to cure cancer. He enlisted the help of longtime ally and former Olympic coach Chris Carmichael, to devise a better strategy. Lance was attempting to do what no one else ever had, and he knew that nothing less than a complete overhaul of his traditional preparation would work.

Chris Carmichael is no stranger to cycling, to the Tour de France, or to Lance Armstrong, for that matter. Carmichael was a member of the 1984 U.S. Olympic cycling team, and later in 1986 was part of the first U.S. team to enter the Tour de France, the legendary 7-Eleven team. Carmichael suffered a career-threatening broken femur that year following the Tour, an injury from which he recovered, only to retire from racing in 1989. Insight gained from his recovery led to his interest in performance coaching, and he began working as development coach for the U.S. cycling team, coaching the 1992 and 1996 Olympic teams. It was in 1990 that he first met the promising cyclist Lance Armstrong, a member of both the '92 and '96 U.S. teams who would in 1993 become the World Champion and in 1995 win a stage in the Tour de France. Throughout the mid-1990s, Carmichael led numerous innovations in training methods and technologies. In 1993, he began to study ways to maximize a rider's power output on the bike, measuring Armstrong's wattage per pedal stroke with road bikes wired with power meters. He then began using wind tunnels to optimize a rider's bike positioning for time trialing, which is a race against the clock, rather than against a competitor. The cover of the June 1996 *Scientific American* featured a cyclist in a wind tunnel, and the accompanying article, written by fellow Olympic coaching member Jay Kearney, featured an in-depth look at the advanced training methods being used in Armstrong's preparation for the Olympics. Armstrong spent hours in the wind tunnel, experimenting with every aspect, including infinitesimal shifts in his body position, seeking the elusive perfect form. In a time trial, every second counts, and a tenth of a second can be the difference between a gold and silver medal. Finding a way to shave off even a hundredth of a second per kilometer grants what could be a winning margin in a forty-kilometer time trial. Innovations in equipment design, clothing material, and pedaling motion were made. It was during this time that Carmichael began to shape his own approach to performance improvement: "At the highest levels of sport, it takes a huge effort to see a one percent improvement in performance, and no individual change in training or nutrition is solely responsible. Rather, it is the combination of minute modifications that leads to significant gains." Former U.S. Olympic cycling team physiologist Edmund Burke, who has written several books, including one with Carmichael, has said that "the genius of Chris is that he understands how much small gains matter. In fact, small gains are all you will ever see." Indeed, at the top echelon of athletic performance, even a *half* percent improvement is significant. Little by little, like Michelangelo releasing David from the marble, they subtracted time and weight from man, machine, and materiel, while increasing speed and power that set new benchmarks across the board. But Carmichael's approach would soon be tested.

As I spoke to Chris, I got the sense that October 2, 1996, was a true turning point for him, a life-changing event for himself and for Armstrong. That was the day Lance was confirmed to have advanced testicular cancer. Chris immediately left his Olympic post to be with Armstrong throughout his treatment and recovery, an event that would not only push his career in new directions, but alter forever his philosophy on elite performance. It was Carmichael who told Lance he could win the Tour de France. They began their work in 1997, when physicians declared Lance cancer-free.

Chris discovered immediately that Armstrong's physiology had changed dramatically: he was twenty pounds lighter, with a much diminished muscle mass. That meant that the way his body most efficiently produced power had changed. What hadn't changed, though, were the demands of winning the Tour, so he needed a new way to ride the bike in order to compete at the elite level. But how many ways could there possibly be to ride a bike?

Carmichael dismantled and rethought the equation of Power = Force × Velocity, where force was the force applied to the pedals and velocity was leg speed, or pedal cadence. He did the math, looking at all the variables. What was the most efficient way for Lance to produce sustainable power, given his newfound physiology and his unique strengths on the bike? If it took 200 watts to move a bike at 20 mph, what were the possibilities? Was there a way to actually generate greater power with less force, *Aikido*-style? A lower cadence using a higher gear ratio required applying greater force to each pedal stroke, which meant more work for Lance's legs, and quicker fatigue. On the other hand, using lower gears spun at a higher cadence required lower force per stroke, but meant more work for his heart and aerobic system. And that was Lance's strength. His resting heartbeat was a mere thirty-two beats per minute, enough to make any physician do a double-take, and his aerobic capacity measured by maximum oxygen uptake was well above that of even those at the top of the cycling field. Given Lance's stronger aerobic engine, Carmichael switched his old climbing technique— the widely accepted practice of driving big gears while seated at around 70 to 75 revolutions per minute—to spinning lower gears at a much higher cadence, around 95 to over 100 revolutions per minute, up out of the saddle to involve more of the supporting muscles. It took months of rigorous practice and training to completely rewire Armstrong's neuromuscular system. The duo worked hard on Lance's pedaling motion to maximize efficiency. It took years to perfect. But by Armstrong's third Tour de France victory, the 2001 Tour, not even the best of the climbing specialists—referred to in cycling lore as "angels of the mountains"—could touch him in the most grueling mountain climbs of the Alps and Pyrenees. After one particularly impressive day, rider Laurent Roux, who had been the early leader of the stage, said afterward, "When he [Lance] passed me, I had the impression that it was a motorcycle at my side. It was beautiful to see." The expert bike technician Lennard Zinn, writing for cycling magazine *VeloNews*, wrote that "Watching his [Armstrong's] feet swing so elegantly through each stroke, ankling from flat to toe-down and back 90 times per minute, is like watching an artist in action." For Lance Armstrong, the elegant solution to the problem of winning the Tour de France was, well, pedaling faster than everyone else. Who knew?

But by 2003, this "new" way to ride the bike had become standard practice in training and racing, and Lance's competitive advantage had dwindled. Armstrong and Carmichael huddled to collaborate on a new way to train in advance of the 2004 Tour. Carmichael rethought the previous year's regimen, and quickly concluded that the old-school training methods lacked specificity, which resulted in inefficient training. Riders would stay in the saddle for six hours or more, but at intensity levels over or under the optimum level needed to yield desired gains. He figured that with more precise goals for each workout, only four hours might be needed to accomplish what once took six. The extra time on the bike wasn't needed or helpful and just led to fatigue and longer recovery periods—it was just plain waste.

At the heart of the new approach was a "stop doing" strategy Jim Collins would surely admire. Carmichael focused directly on the inefficient training and inconsistent dieting. Specially engineered wattage meters designed into the training bike were used to accurately gauge when specific workout goals and power levels had been met. Lance's diet was revamped to match the needs of his training regimen, which provided him with the necessary nutrition for health and performance, without the excess calories that lead to unwanted weight gain. Doing so left more time for Lance to recover better, which in turn allowed higher-intensity training within a much shorter time frame. Lance's simplified preparation also gave him more free time. Eliminating the waste from his program gave him more flexibility to handle his active media schedule without compromising preparation or performance.

What Lance "stopped doing" gave him more power on the bike and the extra edge needed to lead what is arguably the most grueling endurance sports event on the planet. While at the University of Maastricht, Dutch nutritionist Wim H. M. Saris studied human endurance by following the Tour contestants, concluding that "it is without any doubt the most demanding athletic event." In Saris's view, the three-week race is like running twenty-one marathons in as many days. Every cyclist in the Tour burns between seven and ten thousand calories a day. No other event comes close to those levels over a three-week span.

Lance Armstrong went on to win his sixth and seventh consecutive Tour de France victories, a record not likely to be matched in his lifetime. He attributes much of his success to the Carmichael approach. Carmichael and Armstrong changed the game, forever—changing how cyclists approach their sport, how they prepare, how they perform, and how they compete— all through a process of subtraction. For Lance Armstrong, the missing piece, the piece he needed to *make* missing, was a good part of what he was hired to do: ride a bike.

There are some important lessons to be taken from the Carmichael approach. First, the subtractive process of reducing and removing resistance is an effective way to battle our tendency to go overboard in our effort to achieve a goal. Doing more and pushing harder than actually necessary can impede and even reverse progress by introducing overload, inconsistency, and waste. Second, the objective is not to necessarily find a way to do less, but to optimize and maximize the expenditure of one's assets and resources. Doing less in one area may require doing more in another, which is fine if the load is leveled and balanced. In the case of Armstrong's shift in pedal cadence, less force meant greater power, but only when the load from the required faster revolution velocity could be shifted without creating another problem. Third, drastic change isn't always necessary for dramatic results. Making a small subtraction in a thoughtful way can yield an astounding result. To invoke a more familiar sports metaphor, to hit a home run you don't always have to swing for the fence. You have to manage the strike zone and the bat-on-ball contact point. Chris Carmichael was after elegance, and subtraction was his way of accomplishing it.

The Carmichael approach to performance made me wonder whether the same sort of subtractive principles could be applied in the more workaday world of industry.

*c.*

At exactly 12:01 a.m. on Sunday, October 1, 1989, those in the United Kingdom who had not yet nodded off in front of the telly sat straight up in bed as a rather curious message played across their screens:

> Please do not be alarmed. This is the first attempt to communicate across time. This experiment is being sponsored by first direct to celebrate our 21st anniversary; for us, it is the year 2010. To celebrate the 21st anniversary of first direct, we have returned to the date of our launch. We return you now to your programs with best wishes for your personal happiness in your own future.

The provocative commercial, the brainchild of ad agency Howell Henry Childecott Lury, was produced for the launch of first direct (no capital letters, please!), a new bank with an all-new banking concept. Viewers got the message that whatever the new idea was, it was futuristic. What they would soon find out was that first direct was missing a big piece of the conventional banking infrastructure. It was completely without branches. The entire bank was virtual, phone-only. In 1989, that was radical.

One minute before the seductive advertisement ran, the phone lines of first direct had opened to the public. Over the course of the next twenty-four hours, over one thousand calls came in to first direct, calls handled not by newfangled technology or overseas outsourcing, but by real people in first direct's operation headquarters. By the end of the following year, over 60,000 people had become first direct customers. The bank counted nearly ten times that number by the end of 1995, the year it became profitable. The bank has been profitable every year since. How did first direct find virtual success a full decade before the World Wide Web and the cellular phone became everyday appliances?

Project Raincloud was an appropriate name for the special task force chartered in June 1988 by Midland Bank PLC, which along with Barclays, Lloyds, and NatWest was one of the four primary High Street banks in the United Kingdom. (Nearly every town in the U.K. had a High Street, where the large commercial banks had a branch.) The bank was in a world of hurt, having lost over £500 million in the aftermath of some serious write-offs due to some poor acquisitions and several bad loans to developing world countries. The bank's reputation for service was far from sterling, but then the entire retail banking sector in the U.K. during that time suffered the same ailment. The U.K.'s Henley Centre for Forecasting had reported that banks held the lowest marks for service quality out of all retail markets in the United Kingdom. Project Raincloud was challenged with finding an innovative alternative to branch-based banking, one that focused on providing real value to retail banking customers.

At that time, senior management at Midland had become aware of the rising reputation for quality in Japanese goods. In the wake of the severe downturn in the U.S. stock market in 1987, financial institutions such as Fidelity Investments, unable to control returns on investments, had cast about for ways to improve service quality. Edward C. Johnson III, chairman and CEO of Fidelity and a highly regarded financial manager, had gone to school on *Kaizen*, the Japanese word for continuous improvement, inspired by Masaaki Imai's 1986 business management book of the same name. The book positioned *Kaizen* as the key to Japan's competitive success, and attributed Japan's rise from the ruins of World War II to it. Senior management at Midland eventually incorporated *Kai-*

*zen* into their core values, and it became part of the guiding force behind the efforts of Project Raincloud.

*Kaizen* roughly translates to "change for the better." It is at once a principle and a practice. As a principle, *Kaizen* puts creating customer-defined value at the center of all activity. As a practice, *Kaizen* entails just three fairly simple steps: create a standard, follow it, and find a better way. The irony is that while *Kaizen* may be a Japanese word, and responsible for Japan's quality progress, it is an American-made method.

General Douglas MacArthur arrived on Japanese soil in 1945 to begin a seven-year occupation, facing what appeared to be an almost insurmountable challenge: stabilize the country. What he saw was far from stable. Tokyo had been devastated. The economy was in shambles, the industrial base having been literally vaporized. Civil unrest, starvation, Communism, and severe resource constraints in the way of land, facilities, money, and labor skills all threatened the mission of getting Japan back on its feet. MacArthur reached back to Washington to enlist the help of a Roosevelt-created emergency service program called Training Within Industry (TWI). Unfortunately, it wasn't there.

When France fell to Hitler's Third Reich in 1940 and U.S. involvement in the European Theater looked imminent, U.S. factories needed ways not only to ramp up production quickly, but also to rapidly train people to replace the workers who had become soldiers. The Department of War formed TWI to help quickly boost production and productivity. Three programs were developed, and one of them, Job Methods, taught how to generate and implement ideas through hundreds of small changes that could be effected immediately. The term used for the method was *continuous improvement*. The focus was on improving the current work and existing equipment, because there simply wasn't time for large-scale ideas or design of new tools.

Training happened rapidly, using a train-the-trainer, multiplier approach: five course developers each taught two trainers, who in turn trained twenty instructors each. These trainers taught and led "quality circles" in nearly 17,000 plants in America. By the end of the war, TWI had trained nearly two million people.

MacArthur saw TWI as a good way to jump-start the reconstruction effort. But TWI had been discontinued following the end of World War II. Fortunately, one of the original TWI instructors had formed TWI, Inc., and came to support MacArthur's occupation forces. By 1953, the approach had become Japan's de facto standard business practice and had been customized and incorporated into nearly every major manufacturing operation in the country. Japan made continuous improvement all their own, dubbing it *Kaizen.*

According to the *Kaizen* view, there are two types of work: value-adding and non-value-adding. Anything that doesn't add value for someone somewhere should be targeted for reduction or removal, because the stated goal of *Kaizen* is to constantly improve the tangible drivers of value: quality, cost, and delivery speed. In the *Kaizen* view, the best way to do that is to eliminate to the best of your ability the things that hurt quality, raise costs, and slow things down—exactly the kinds of things that In-N-Out has generally been able to avoid, and what Chris Carmichael targeted to improve Lance Armstrong's performance. In other words, it is the laws of subtraction that guide *Kaizen.*

The words *muri, mura,* and *muda* in Japanese hold a special place in the heart of a well-trained *Kaizen* practitioner. They are the contribution to the practice of *Kaizen* by Taiichi

Ohno, the founding engineer of the Toyota Production System in manufacturing. *Muri* means overload, and is described as stress, strain, or undercapacity. *Mura* means inconsistency, and can take the form of irregularity, imbalance, or interruption. *Muda* means waste, and comes in seven basic flavors: overproduction, waiting, defects, overprocessing, and any unnecessary motion, inventory, or transportation. *Muda* is the easiest to target because it is generally more visible. But *muri* and *mura* are often the more evil of the sins, as they can be the actual cause of all *muda*. The Project Raincloud team found all three—*muri, mura, muda*—in all their many forms, in the course of conducting their research, at the branches of Midland Bank.

As the team talked to their current customer base, they were surprised to discover that a fifth hadn't been to a branch in the past month, much less in the past week. Nearly half had never met their branch manager, and over 40 percent said they'd rather not visit the branch at all, thank you very much, unless they absolutely had to. When it got right down to it, the most common financial transactions—like making deposits, paying bills, getting cash—didn't require face-to-face contact. The ones that did, like getting a loan, had extremely low volume. That raised the rather glaring question: Why do we need branches anyway? One answer was that people still believed personal attention and service were very important. But could that be provided through means other than a branch visit, a trip that was at the time not even on the monthly to-do list of the average customer?

What the team came to understand was that their customers defined value in three ways: information, communication, and trust. These were the necessary ingredients for any personal banking relationship. They realized that the third element, that of trust, was an outcome of the quality, cost, and delivery speed of the first two. Information and communication could be provided in a high-quality, high-speed, low-cost way through a combination of technology and well-trained personnel who were always available and responsive. Not only were information, communication, and trust the very elements missing from the bank branch, but a branch added no value in the customer's mind. Project Raincloud concluded that branches could be eliminated altogether, believing that not only would service quality rise, profits would too. If they could replicate a personal banking relationship built on information, communication, and trust over phone lines on a large scale and at a fraction of the cost of a branch system, that value would flow to stockholders and customers alike.

Midland Bank formed a subsidiary, and Project Raincloud became the basis for the new concept, to be branded as first direct. It was indeed the "first direct" bank. The other High Street banks pooh-poohed the idea that anyone would consider telephone-only banking. But by 1996, first direct had over 650,000 customers, two-thirds of whom had abandoned the High Street banks, Midland included. A 1992 television commercial featured an actor portraying a first direct customer saying, "I've never actually seen the people at first direct. But I believe, I really believe, they exist." A real customer, a risk management director at a London investment house who had switched from High Street bank NatWest to first direct during its launch, told researchers from Harvard Business School, "I was fed up with the slow service at the local bank branches. First direct's service is very good and always open—24 hours a day and 365 days a year. Their people are knowledgeable and friendly. Their rates are competitive and they have a good product range. I've referred about ten of my friends to bank with first direct."

It seems the commercial that played on that early Sunday morning nearly twenty-one years ago was a self-fulfilling prophecy. Today, first direct continues its success story, flourishing in a Web and cellular world. They now have over 1.2 million customers, and nearly 900,000 of them use Internet banking. Nearly 400,000 use SMS text messaging banking; in fact, first direct is the largest text messaging bank in the UK, sending around 2.6 million text messages to customers every month. The 2,800 customer service experts in first direct's two corporate locations handle 235,000 telephone calls every week, over 13,000 calls a day outside working hours, and over 500 calls a day from abroad. With onsite masseur, concierge, car servicing, and laundry to name but a few of the services provided to its 3,400 employees, it's not too surprising that first direct was named to the 2006 *Sunday Times* 100 Best Companies to Work For list. The success of first direct certainly raises the question of why branches at other major banks have not gone the way of the dinosaurs.

For me, the story of first direct raised the question of what other kinds of operations and structures might be subtracted to improve performance.

*d.*

A tree probably centuries old grows in the middle of the walkway leading up to the French company known only as FAVI, a small fifty-year-old designer and manufacturer of copper alloy automotive components. The path was clearly designed around the tree. Jean-François Zobrist, FAVI's chief executive officer, uses the tree as a working metaphor for FAVI's mission—to maintain enough growth and profitability over the long haul to stay alive, not necessarily to be the biggest. FAVI is located in the small village of Hallencourt, in the Picardy region of France, just a bit over a hundred miles outside of Paris to the north. When you drive through the countryside of Picardy, you feel as if you're looking at what surely must be the field location used to film every World War I and World War II movie you've ever seen. There are Gothic cathedrals and castles that tower over the rolling greens, and tiny hamlets that are neat and inviting. This tranquil farm country is the site of some of the worst battles in history. The Somme River cuts through Picardy, and the Battle of the Somme was one of the largest and bloodiest battles of World War I, with over one million casualties. But the people of Picardy have endured many wars and invasions. In fact, if you were to explore an older farmhouse, you would likely find a secret trapdoor somewhere behind the chimney that leads to a room underneath the house, where the family might have hidden while enemy soldiers passed through. And that's why the tree remains where it can't possibly be missed, in the center of the walk every employee must make from their car to their station. It's not only a reminder to place growth and survival foremost in one's mind, but also of the importance Picardy people place on staying put, having weathered the worst of wartimes.

FAVI first came to my attention through a short article in the *Wall Street Journal.* What caught my eye and prompted me to seek an audience with Monsieur Zobrist was that FAVI, a company that employed nearly six hundred people, had gone without a personnel department for over two decades. It was one of the first things Jean-François removed when he took the helm in 1983. As I was to soon find out, that wasn't all he eliminated.

There aren't many CEOs who will proclaim, "I am a stupid and lazy manager," much less do so right up front in the conversation. Usually that sort of revelation is reserved for events outside working hours. Of course, this was Jean-François's way of explaining why he puts the company in the hands of the people doing the work. "I have no idea of what people are doing," he says. What he means is that he does not possess the expertise to do their work, so he should therefore have no input into it. His job, as he sees it, is to "be the headlights and the windshield" of the vehicle that is FAVI, acting as the guiding light and provider of vision. FAVI is as unique as Jean-François, and different from any other factory I've ever been to, and I've been to many. It's missing many things.

It's true that FAVI has no personnel department. In fact, there is no structural hierarchy *anywhere* at FAVI. There is no middle management, no central operating committees, no time clocks or cards, and no thick employee handbooks jammed with the traditional "do this, don't do that" policies. No one at FAVI uses the words *personnel, worker,* or *employee.* (And not because they're English words, either.) As far as Jean-François is concerned, nearly all of the conventions of the modern organization don't make much sense, and to him, centralizing departments and functions only serves to impose "arbitrary restrictions on people's activity and swell their own ranks to police those constraints." The central chain-of-command structure is definitely a big piece of what is missing from the FAVI culture. But it hasn't always been this way.

The culture at FAVI when Jean-François came on the scene was just the opposite. If you wanted a tool, for example, you had to go to the person in charge of monitoring time cards, who kept the tools under tight security and who seemed to take a rather perverse pleasure in penalizing people for being late. If it was a hot summer day, you might find the windows closed as employees suffered in the unhealthy swelter of the metal foundry to earn a "heat premium" in their wages given for keeping the temperature above a certain threshold. The central planning committee spent two hours a week going over why production was yet again behind and deliveries were late, yet spent no time on the actual planning activity itself.

By the time he was given the leadership of FAVI, Jean-François had grown weary of what he terms the *chaine de comment*. The best way to translate this is "chain of how." In the *chaine de comment* system, he says, "everyone is stupid except the CEO. If you ask the operator, he says, 'I don't know, talk to my supervisor.' Then you go to the supervisor, and he says, 'I don't know, talk to the shop boss.' But the shop boss doesn't know. Neither does the director, who says, 'Talk to the CEO.' " So what Jean-François did was to turn the *chaine de comment* system on its ear. "Now it is the CEO—me—who is stupid," he smiles, using the phrase *"Il faut laisser le 'comment' à ceux qui font"*—leave the how-to to those who actually do the job. This is the foundation of *Kaizen*.

What's so fascinating about FAVI is that not only is it an extremely flat organization located in a country fond of centralization and thriving in a fiercely competitive and mature industry, but the change from the old FAVI to the new happened literally overnight. I was expecting to hear all about the big "change management" effort that was required to shift to an autonomous operation, how much time it took, how costly it was, and how much resistance had to be overcome. I was shocked when Jean-François relayed how he did it. "I came in the day after I became CEO, and gathered the people. I told them tomorrow when you come to work, you do not work for me or for a boss. You work for your customer. I don't pay you. They do. Every customer has its own factory now. You do what is needed for the customer." And with that, he dismantled and destroyed the central departments and organizational chart: personnel, gone; product development, gone; purchasing, gone. Jean-François Zobrist broke all the rules of the management game. So how *does* it work?

Approximately twenty teams were formed on the spot, based on knowledge of the customer: Fiat, Volvo, Volkswagen, etc. Each team was responsible not only for the customer, but for its own human resources, purchasing, and product development. There are two job designations in the team: leader and *compagnon*—or companion—which is an operator able to perform several different jobs. Every customer has a single FAVI linchpin, who oversees all aspects of the relationship, which are handled by the team, including all of the technical requirements, cost negotiations, purchasing, product development, quality control issues, scheduling and delivery, meeting organization, and information coordinating. The linchpin is a critical position of high strategic importance, so Jean-François handpicked each one. In effect, what happened at FAVI was that it moved from being one big plant to being a couple of dozen entrepreneurial miniplants housed under one roof, with a "no policy" policy.

The lack of hierarchy solves a number of problems. With work at FAVI organized into horizontal customer teams, job titles and promotions become irrelevant, so they are no longer a distraction. All that energy is channeled into the work itself, which at FAVI is of the highest quality. Accountability is to the customer and to the team, not a boss—FAVI people are free to experiment, innovate, and solve problems for customers. They're known for working off-shift to serve customers or to test out new procedures. Equipment, tooling, workspace, and process redesign all rest in the hands of those doing the work. FAVI people are encouraged to make decisions and take quick action to improve their daily work and respond to the needs of their customers. Control rests with the front lines, where it adds the most value. As for Jean-François, he spends a great deal of his time ignoring the "how," choosing instead to communicate purpose—the "who" and "why" message of serving customers. He has but one demand of his people, and it is a familiar one for a *Kaizen* practitioner: faster, better, cheaper, smarter . . . for the customer.

It works. FAVI's teams are known for extreme responsiveness. During a strike by the French teamsters that closed major roads at the French border and threatened to delay on-time deliveries to a longtime German customer, the FAVI team took it upon themselves to map out a contingency plan to avoid being stopped at the roadblocks. Using backroads and small trucks, they were able to make all deliveries as scheduled.

Still, customers visiting FAVI are often astounded at what they perceive to be a total lack of control. A favorite story Jean-François tells involves a customer's site inspection at FAVI: "They asked to audit our procedures," he says. "They were not pleased because we had no measurement system for tracking late orders—nothing in place, no plan, no process, no structure in case of delay. They are a customer for over ten years, so I say, 'In that time, have we ever been late?' They say, 'No.' I say, 'Have we ever been early?' They say again, 'No.' And so I ask them why they want me to measure things that do not exist." Good point.

Not only does FAVI maintain a strong double-digit profitability, it does so in markets where its competitors either lose money or slash production costs through Asian outsourcing. And it consistently lowers its prices. For example, the cost to produce a copper gearbox fork—a major transmission component—is nearly half what it was twenty years ago, thanks to the efforts of the FAVI autonomous team approach.

Not everyone is fortunate enough to work for a firm like FAVI that believes in the power of people or trusts them implicitly. And perhaps you're thinking that Jean-François, being the CEO, owns the house, so he can do whatever he wants. Is there, then, an example that is a bit closer to home for nearly everyone? There is, quite literally so.

*e.*

There is a house in the suburbs of Minneapolis that, as you approach it, gives you a sense that something a bit out of the ordinary is waiting for you inside. It's mysterious but welcoming. There's a big front-facing gable, and the high roof cantilevers out over the front and back of the first floor with eaves that overhang the sides by a good five feet. It looks like a safe and solid shelter. Something about the front porch and deep entry to the front door makes you feel like you've entered the house before you actually have. As you step across the threshold and enter the house into a small receiving area, it takes all of a blink of an eye to notice a number of things missing from what most people think of when their "dream house" comes to mind. First of all, there is no cathedral ceiling, and no grand foyer where your guests can wait as you descend down the sweeping spiral staircase . . . that isn't there. There is no great room, no formal living room, and no formal dining room. There is just enough space for two or three people to talk for a moment as you make the transition from public to private space, and much of the first floor is visible the moment you step inside. Your eyes are drawn straight through the house on the long view to a light from a window in the door at the other end of the house. The kitchen, dining area, and living area are all somehow distinct, but not separate. You immediately feel at ease, like there's an enormous amount of space in which to, well, live and breathe—just *be*—because there is a distinctive lack of complete walls, which have been replaced by various structures that merely suggest the separation of what is essentially a quadrant of open space. Every space seems to flow into the next. Two long, dropped soffits run the length and breadth of the house and divide the plan into four sections, allowing each its own identity. Columns are placed where the soffits intersect, which further helps to define the different spaces while obviously providing structural support. So, while it's clear which areas are for dining and living, they merge with the kitchen, which, as anyone who's hosted a party or has children can tell you, is generally where everyone ends up anyway.

There is just one fully enclosed area, a rather cozy-looking "away room" meant for escape, solitude, study, sleeping, or sending little ones to watch the *SpongeBob SquarePants* movie for the millionth time. All throughout the house in what are usually empty corners and wasted space in most homes are alcoves and built-in shelves. At the top of the stairs, for example, there is a desk built into the space below the ship's ladder to the attic, which gives a sense of shelter and seems like the perfect spot for kids to do homework or play computer games. The attic itself is a windowed loft in the peak of the roof that adds another living dimension, becoming perhaps a place where the teens in the family can escape to without leaving the house and stirring up trouble.

Functional beauty abounds, and many spaces pull double duty. For example, flanking the fireplace in what is usually reserved for a nonfunctional hearth are comfortable window seats. In the master bedroom is a walk-in closet just big enough to double as a dressing room. With enough space for dressers, mirrors, shelves, a chair, and several rows of hanging clothes, it's behind a door, so you can dress for your 4 a.m. fishing expedition without waking everyone in the house.

Ceiling and floor heights and shapes vary, which keeps your eyes roving, as do the myriad bold colors used. There seems to be a massive amount of light, which is due not only to the many windows and see-through spaces that effectively bring the outside in, but also the many surfaces that are covered with various reflecting materials and that do what mirrors do—give the illusion of more space.

Standing in the shared space of the first floor, you get the feeling you're in a house that must easily be thirty-five hundred square feet. You're not. The entire home is all of two thousand square feet. This is the *Life* magazine Dream House of 1999, designed by architect Sarah Susanka. As it first did in 1938 when it commissioned Frank Lloyd Wright to design a perfect dream home, *Life* invited her to be its chosen architect following the overwhelming success of her 1998 book *The Not So Big House: A Blueprint for the Way We Really Live.* It is indeed a Not So Big House.

I first met Sarah Susanka at the 2007 Pacific Coast Builders Conference, a gigantic weeklong affair of trade shows, presentations, and seminars consuming all four exhibit halls of San Francisco's Moscone Center. As I listened to her keynote address, it became clear that Sarah has redefined the way we should think about the most important material possession we may own.

A Not So Big House, which, in reality, is not necessarily small, is defined as one that is simply not as big as you think you need, because it is tailored to the way you actually live. The average square footage of a house in the United States has grown from 1,400 square feet in the late 1960s to nearly 2,400 square feet in 2005, but on average, a third of the space in most homes is never used. How often do we use our nicely appointed formal dining and living rooms? Certainly not nearly full-time.

Not true in a Not So Big House, in which *all* the space gets lived in *all* the time, and which is likely to be a third smaller than a conventional home that's based on thinking that is no longer relevant. "We live far more casually than we used to," says Sarah, "but it's as if we still live in the formality of the Victorian age. It's as if visitors are presented with a stage set, while the people who live there spend their time backstage."

The magic, as clients of Sarah's will tell you, is that although the house is smaller in square footage, it actually feels much bigger. I interviewed George Knopfler, an attorney in Southern California who a few years ago moved his practice from rural Santa Ynez to more urban Thousand Oaks. He told me that the nearly 8,000-square-foot house he now occupies in a very exclusive gated community "is half the size" of the 4,000-square-foot home—quite large by Sarah's standards and a project that George had to twist her arm to undertake—that Sarah designed for him in 1996. George's wife, Debbie, told me not to make her "think about the Susanka house, it'll just make me cry," and as I left their current mansion, George gestured toward the second floor, saying, "See all that? We never go up there." A Not So Big House is one that uses less space to give a greater quality of life, dispensing with the spaces rarely used and that may "detract from the soul of the home."

That's a fundamentally different view of what a house should be and do. By taking a "build better, not bigger" approach, focusing on quality over quantity, Sarah can design a home to reflect how you really live—how you like to inhabit space, how you spend your time, and what makes you feel comfortable. She views her role as not really minimizing anything, but as maximizing her client's dream, and dollar, by creating a space with substance and spirit, all of which is in use every day. But by doing that, she indirectly minimizes the waste and overload in the typical house.

"When it comes to picking a house, we seem to have forgotten a very important third dimension," she tells me. "We look at a two-dimensional floorplan, which tells us little about what it's like to live there." If you think about it, that's like picking the city, town, and neighborhood you're going to live in by looking at an aerial view of it on Google maps. "We don't buy cars that way," she says, "so why something even more important, our house! Not only that, but we generally don't buy the very biggest car we can afford. We buy a car based on many other factors. It's not just about square footage."

As an architectural student, Sarah was greatly influenced by the work of noted architectural design theorist Christopher Alexander, professor emeritus at the University of California, Berkeley. His 1977 tome *A Pattern Language* remains Sarah's personal handbook. Alexander reasoned that users know more about the kind of building they need than any architect could, and he set out to discover and validate the timeless principles inherent in the most enduring structures and spaces, irrespective of scale. Gathering input from international students and faculty, Alexander conducted an in-depth global survey of the design principles of architecture, from city plans down to individual rooms. He identified over two hundred patterns, and rendered them in the book in a way even Donald Knuth would admire. (*A Pattern Language* has indeed found its way into the world of computer programming.) The patterns have distinct ties to the fractal patterns of nature. For example, many of the medieval towns and cities Alexander observed are visually pleasing, balanced, and harmonious in design, with rooms in houses similar in pattern to the larger home, and buildings similar in pattern to the overall city, something he explained by noting that they were not built to a central plan, but to local building codes that mandated a few required features, but freed the builder to interpret them and adapt them to the specific situation as desired and appropriate. In another pattern, Alexander maintained that above four stories, people lose connection with the street below, so if you want a vibrant village, a simple rule is to limit building height to four levels.

In his follow-up book, *The Timeless Way of Building*, Alexander set forth the ultimate aspiration of any structure:

> There is one timeless way of building. It is a thousand years old, and the same today as it has ever been. The great traditional buildings of the past, the villages and tents and temples in which man feels at home, have always been made by people who were very close to the center of this way. It is not possible to make great buildings, or great towns, beautiful places, places where you feel yourself, places where you feel alive, except by following this way. And, as you will see, this way will lead anyone who looks for it to buildings which are themselves as ancient in their form, as the trees and hills, and as our faces are.

So what is that quality? Alexander calls it a "creative unfolding," yet a "quality without a name."

Sarah Susanka came face-to-face with this nameless quality at the beginning of her career. Her very first client, an elderly woman who had embraced what she called "sensibilities of Japanese aesthetics," introduced Sarah to the word *shibui*, which is the adjective form of the noun *shibumi*. Sarah is accurate in her description of it:

> In Japanese, the word *shibui* is used to describe a quality of design that many Not So Big Houses possess. It can be an elusive concept to grasp, however, because we have nothing similar in our language. Words that combine to give a sense of its meaning include *simplicity, elegance, beauty, functionality, restraint, reserve, refinement,*

and *quietude.* The term can apply to anything that has been designed, from an article of clothing to a piece of furniture to a building. But none of these words describe how this quality comes into being. Though something *shibui* looks effortlessly simple, even inevitable, it takes much labor and refinement to reach this state. The quality of *shibumi* evolves out of a process of complexity, though none of this complexity shows in the result. It often seems to arise when an architect is striving to meet a particular design challenge. When you stop to think back on houses that have made an impact on you, they'll often be the ones where an awkward problem has been cleverly solved in a way that makes you think, "Well of course! How else could it be?" When something has been designed really well, it has an understated, effortless beauty, and it really works. That's simply *shibui.*

I asked Sarah to take me back to when the Not So Big notion began to crystallize in her mind. As she expanded her practice through the 1980s and 1990s, she began to notice something that intrigued her. Her superwealthy clients did not build formal living rooms or formal dining rooms. *Ever.* But her more middle-income clients demanded both. *Always.* It didn't make sense, at least not immediately. What was behind this rather marked difference?

"It finally dawned on me," she tells me, "that the design motivations were completely different, and had nothing to do with actual people or lifestyle differences. The superwealthy could afford to build exactly what they wanted. You'd think they would want those formal spaces for all the entertaining they did. But they didn't, because they didn't do any more entertaining than the rest of us. That's an incorrect stereotype. Income equals formality isn't a foregone conclusion. The motivation for the middle-income client, though, was *resale*. Appraisers and agents had them convinced that if they wanted to someday sell their home, they absolutely must have a formal living room and dining room. The superwealthy simply didn't care about resale. That was the lightbulb. The really obvious thing was that 99 percent of us simply don't have enough money to accomplish what we think we want. Unless we take something out, we can't do it. The Not So Big House arose out of absolute need... if I wanted to help make a dream come true, I had to find a big chunk of cost to take out. Ironically, my wealthiest clients showed me the way."

Sarah's battle was mostly uphill, except of course with her wealthy clientele, until the publication of *The Not So Big House* in 1998 and the *Life* magazine Dream House commission in 1999. So just what are some of the design concepts at play, and where do they meet up with symmetry, seduction, and the laws of subtraction?

Sarah is in the business of creating an experience by shaping space. When we think of space, we generally think about it in terms of quantity of volume: not enough space or lots of space. But it's not volume we're really after, it's what that volume can do for us, or how it can make us feel. It needs to accommodate how we live. The design of many homes focuses one-dimensionally on volume, a view that neglects what the physicists we have met would say is inseparable from space: time. Sarah calls the volume focus a "potter's view." A potter is concerned with shaping clay into a container, which puts the focus on the outside, not the space within. Taking the same view in the design of a living space ignores the fact that we spend time *in* the space. When you shape space with time in mind, the symmetrical and seductive aspects of elegance open themselves up to a subtractive approach that results in more of what you really want: an engaging experience.

One step inside the *Life* magazine Dream House, you're met with a view that is indeed intriguing. What draws you into the space is the partially hidden view of the living, dining, and kitchen areas, which makes you want to see more. We want to satisfy our curiosity and to fill in the gap created by the incomplete walls.

Moving into the main space, you realize that it is a sequence of connected spaces, rather than a set of discrete rooms. "What's important to understand here," Sarah explains, "is that we experience space not just by quantity alone, but the interconnections between one bit of space and another." What makes this living area different from, say, a conventional great room, is the use of varying ceiling heights to identify one place from the next, without using walls. None of the spaces have a particularly high ceiling, yet each one is clearly a separate activity place, and all of them work together.

Varying the ceiling height is a key design concept used throughout the house to sculpt the various rooms and to perform triple duty: separation, connection, and effectiveness. The mudroom that connects the garage to the house, for example, has coat-hanging and mail-sorting places that are differentiated from the hallway by a dropped ceiling that gives each function a discrete identity, along with a sense of shelter. Without that change in ceiling height, the mudroom would be just another run-of-the-mill back entrance, without much in the way of personality. It's the way the room has been divided into several parts that makes it more appealing.

Ceiling height variation is a simple example of how effective subtraction can be in creating an engaging experience. In fact, one of the first things Susanka taught me was how to subtract two from one to get three. That's not bad math, that's good architecture. Here's how it works. Suppose I gave you a rectangular room—your basic ceiling, floor, and walls—that looks like this from the side:

Can you subtract two blocks of space to turn the room into three rooms? All you have to do is drop the ceiling height in two places, and you will have created the visual perception of three distinct spaces.

You can subtract even more space to better define the separation by varying the floor heights. Along with using partial walls, this is the architectural version of exploiting the brain's filling-in talent. When you divide space this way into discrete but visible areas, your brain not only closes the gap, but also tells you there's more there. This was a trick all the clever moms and dads on my block played on us at Halloween. Until I got older and wiser, five sticks of gum always seemed a better prize than a single pack. I now regularly use this tactic on my six-year-old daughter, who, when asked how many pieces of cinnamon toast she wants for breakfast, invariably answers "four!" One slice cut into four squares takes care of her demand quite nicely.

Finally, the Dream House has a certain repetitive rhythm to it. The house has a signature pattern: squares. The whole structure is a square, divided into squares, with variations on the theme that appear throughout—smaller and smaller, self-similar geometrical figures, down to small squares that form part of the lattice on either side of a window bay. It's fractal, in other words. Most houses do not use this kind of symmetry as an organizing feature, and yet it not only allows a continuous flow from one space to another without interruption, but also lets you know that no matter where you are in the house, it's one connected, cohesive whole. In fact, standing in the main intersection of the house might remind you of the shared space of Laweiplein. Perhaps achieving elegance begins much closer to home than I originally thought.

The laws of subtraction show how important it is to distinguish between an ingenious subtraction and a simplistic incision. Certainly it takes no genius to make simple cuts—cutting a cost or paring a budget does not constitute the subtractive quality of elegance. That thought raises an important question: Is there a means by which we can continually tap into the power of the missing piece? The counterintuitive approach of the innovators we've met so far reveals a different way of thinking. They are asking questions like: What would my customers love for me to eliminate or reduce or stop adding? What is it that my competition would struggle with if I were to cease? What would those who matter most love for me to stop doing?

In other words, they are studying the board and choosing to play chess, not checkers. We need to unpack that thought process a bit to understand how to use it more in our own efforts. It would help to have a handrail or two to guide our use of the lessons gleaned from our travels through symmetry, seduction, and subtraction—something we can use to better achieve the uncommon simplicity and surprising power of an elegant solution. Does such a strategy exist, and if so, what might it be?

# CHAPTER FIVE

# On Sustainable Solutions

W HEN STANFORD PROFESSOR emeritus Donald Knuth, who as you may recall helped us define the elements of elegance, listed "the immortal ring of an $E=mc^2$" as his final criterion, he was referring to the timeless aspect of Einstein's theory of relativity. That most famous equation has maintained its integrity for over a century, far outlived its creator, and continued to spur study and galvanize thought. In fact, the concept has been strengthened over time as it holds up under close scrutiny and competing theories. In other words, the equation is elegant not only in its uncommon simplicity, but in its sustainability.

Like symmetry, sustainability is easier to describe than to define. Most people think of sustainability in the context of the rising environmental awareness and corporate social responsibility efforts, which focus on ways to make better use of limited, shrinking, and in some cases already scarce raw planetary resources. But this is simply one application of the sustainability principle.

Sustainability can be defined broadly as the ability to maintain something at a certain level, indefinitely. While the definition is easy to grasp, more subtle are two important implications. The first is that to be sustainable, any given asset, no matter what it is, must be kept whole, without making significant trade-offs that undermine the capital used to generate and maintain it. The second follows from the first: sustainability hinges on the ability to see finite resources as the very source of innovation. This insight brings to the fore the creative tension at the center of elegance: achieving the maximum effect with the minimum effort.

From the lasting impact of *The Sopranos'* non-ending to the indelible effect of the letter *E* exercise; from the self-similar symmetries of Jackson Pollock's fractal drippings to the uncontrolled yet highly ordered shared space of Laweiplein; from the ambiguous *Mona Lisa* smile to the absentee iPhone marketing; from the long-secret menu at In-N-Out Burger to the precision training techniques of Chris Carmichael; from the success of the branchless first direct bank and delayered FAVI to the trim fit of a Not So Big House, the stories and examples highlighting the various facets of symmetry, seduction, and subtraction have all had an element of sustainability to them. It is the ability to simultaneously achieve all four factors that makes the surprising ingenuity behind these stories worth exploring.

Whether it's a personal or professional pursuit, we each face the challenge of sustainability at some point, for the simple reason that each day we have more to do and less to do it with. There is little choice but to become more resourceful. Achieving elegance demands that we meet that challenge in a way that avoids causing further complications. But that can be fiendishly difficult, which helps explain why so many well-intentioned solutions are plagued by unwanted side effects or unintended consequences. So while it is this enduring quality that consummates elegance, it can be the most elusive.

To reveal just why that's so, it helps to first look at a cleverly sustainable idea, then try our own hand at a problem requiring similar thinking.

*a.*

The impoverished economy in the rural scrublands of northern Nigeria is based on subsistence farming. The large population inhabiting the many isolated communities survives by growing, consuming, and selling fruits and vegetables nourished by the many streams and rivers that flow into Lake Chad. The arid heat of the semidesert geography presents a significant problem: rapid food decay. Perishables last no more than a few days before spoiling. The solution would seem easy enough: refrigeration. But the problem is far more complex than simply being too poor to afford a refrigerator. For starters, there is no electricity.

For Mohammed Bah Abba, a Nigerian-born business lecturer at Jigawa State Polytechnic in Dutse, close to the nation's northern frontier, the problem seemed even more far-reaching. As a part-time adviser throughout the 1990s to the regional office of the United Nations Development Programme in Jigawa, Abba's work took him into the field, where his daily contact with the community allowed him to closely observe the extreme hardship and widespread suffering. The women of this predominantly polygamist society are segregated from the men and confined to their homes—a cultural practice called purdah. As a result, the young girls of the family were forced to travel long distances to larger markets each day to sell the food as soon as it was harvested, leaving little if any time for school. Time being of the essence, much of what was produced was sold cheap or wasted, resulting in loss to an already meager income, or sold in a partly spoiled state, resulting in health hazards. To Abba, the entire health, welfare, and education of his people appeared to be tied to the inability to keep produce fresh. He set about finding some small way to ease their life, without, he said, "destroying the dignity of purdah." Although Abba was neither inventor nor entrepreneur, he knew that whatever he came up with would have to cost nearly nothing to construct and maintain, work without electricity, use readily available materials and existing skills, and be acceptable in a conservative Muslim community. In short, he would have to think inside a very small box to find a viable solution.

Being from a family of potters, Abba remembered from his youth the clay pots that had in the past been so central to the lives of northern Nigerians. Once used for everything from cooking to coffins, clay pots had been replaced by more modern aluminum and plastic containers. But they hadn't disappeared entirely, and neither had the indigenous skills used to shape them. He remembered the basics of traditional claywork that his grandmother had taught him. And he remembered enough of his secondary school science to hit upon an idea: cooling by evaporation.

You don't need to be a physicist to know that a dog pants heavily to lose heat through the rapid breath flowing over its tongue, or that as sweat evaporates from your skin, you cool off. It's why we might feel cooler in the high but dry heat of a desert climate than in the cooler but much more humid environment of a rain forest. Evaporation is nature's way of dropping the temperature a few degrees. Abba's idea? Clay pots. Or rather, *double* clay pots.

The solution couldn't be simpler. Place one clay pot inside another. Fill the gap with something moist enough to keep both pots damp: wet river sand. Cover the inner pot with a wet cloth. As the moisture in the gap evaporates from the outer pot toward the dry outside air, the inner pot cools. The wet sand plays the dual role of insulating the inner pot. The drop in temperature of several degrees chills the contents of the inner pot, and kills potentially harmful microorganisms that flourish only at higher temperatures. Fruits and vegetables get preserved. Problem solved, with uncommon simplicity and surprisingly sustainable power.

Abba's pot-in-pot desert cooler kept contents a dozen degrees cooler than the surrounding air. In one of his first trials, eggplants stayed fresh for nearly a month instead of three days, and peppers and tomatoes stayed ripe for three weeks. Spinach lasted twelve days instead of spoiling within twenty-four hours.

On his lecturer's salary, Abba set up potteries—the kilns being open fires—employed local potters, and distributed the first 5,000 pots free of charge. A pot cost less than a dollar to make, and could be sold for just about ten cents over cost. A potter, Abba discovered, could make about five complete desert coolers per day.

Today, farmers and traders use the desert coolers to store their produce at home and sell them fresh at a good price to the 100,000 people at the Dutse market. In one interview Abba said, "Farmers are now able to sell on demand rather than 'rush sell' because of spoilage, and income levels have noticeably risen. Married women also have an important stake in the process, as they can sell food from their homes and overcome their age-old dependency on their husbands as the sole providers." They make soft drinks—called *zobo*—and sell them from the coolers. The extra income is used to buy soap and other essentials. The invention frees young girls to attend school, because they no longer have to worry about traveling far and wide to sell food every day.

Abba's solution, which he refined over the course of two years (one prototype used foam from an old mattress instead of sand), captured the attention of the world and received numerous awards and accolades. By 2006, well over 100,000 desert coolers had been sold and distributed all over Nigeria. In Eritrea, just north of Ethiopia on the eastern side of the African continent, an adapted version of Abba's cooler was developed under his advisement and is being used to preserve insulin vials for diabetic patients in remote rural areas.

Mrs. Rabi Umar, secretary of the State Ministry of Women Affairs and Social Mobilization in Nigeria, says that "the pot-in-pot project is the first to use simple cultural solutions to address the primary needs of the rural northern Nigerian population, for whom the basic necessities of life are nearly non-existent."

In awarding Mohammed Bah Abba the 2001 Shell Award for Sustainable Development, the judges' statement said, in part: "Using simple evaporation principles, the earthenware 'pot in pot' cooling system has overcome many of the problems faced by isolated rural communities by preventing the rapid decay of food ... helping to reduce disease, poverty, migration and unemployment, and has benefited local communities by creating skilled workers, raising family incomes, increasing access to education for girls, and allowing women

greater involvement in the community. This remarkably effective design is simple, easy to use, cheap to buy and maintain, and only uses generational skill."

Clay, sand, cloth, water. Mohammed Bah Abba's world-
changing desert cooler is a good example of how resource constraints can spark an ingeniously sustainable solution that solves
many difficult problems at once. Given the low-tech nature of
Abba's idea, it stretches the imagination to think that the solution has only recently been developed. But this kind of simple
elegance is often only obvious in retrospect. It remains to be
shown just how difficult it can be to devise such a clever idea.

### *b.*

Imagine for a moment that you are the manager of the local
video rental store, a branch of a large and successful nationwide chain, many years ago. Back then, a VCR machine did
not have the automatic rewind feature on it. DVDs had not
been invented yet. In other words, if you were to fall asleep
watching the movie, you'd have to hit rewind yourself to start
it over. Your store has a problem: roughly a third of your
customers do not rewind the tape. It is clearly in the contract
that all videos must be rewound. Still, each morning when
you open, your employees report one out of three tapes in
the convenient customer drop box has not been rewound.
According to surveys, this situation is a great source of customer dissatisfaction—the "conscientious rewinders" who
happen to rent a tape that hasn't been rewound aren't happy.
You have tried a number of things to solve the problem: incentives, penalties, "be kind, rewind" reminders, and you've

even put in a bank of five rewind machines for the techno crowd who state that rewinding tapes ruins the tape heads on their VCR. Nothing you've tried has improved the situation. So you ask your employees to help solve the problem. You give them several nonnegotiable conditions, however. First, the solution must achieve a level of 100 percent customer rewind accountability—it's the customer's responsibility, not the store's. Second, there can be no additional burden on the customer. Third, any solution must be of extremely low, and preferably no, cost—mere pennies per tape, at most. Finally, the solution must be easy to implement, without disrupting the normal operation of the store. You tell your employees that you trust their creativity, and that they are free to be as innovative as they wish, as long as all conditions are met.

Try your hand at solving the problem. If you wish, put the book down for ten minutes and let your mind play with the possibilities. What you're looking for is a simple and sustainable solution that fits within the limitations imposed by the four conditions. The rest of this chapter will have much more resonance if you take a stab at it. Enlist the help of someone nearby if you like—sometimes it's easier to brainstorm together. With any luck you've been seduced into cracking the problem. Keep in mind what you've discovered about elegance to this point. (Oh, and don't frustrate yourself trying to invent autorewind VCRs and DVDs—not only will you violate the conditions of the challenge, but they aren't necessary to solve the problem.)

•    ◦    ◦

This problem is based on the story of video chain Star Video, which solved the problem elegantly. I turned the story into a thought exercise and since 2005 I have given it to over 25,000 people in lectures and workshops. The results are always the same, irrespective of the size or makeup of the group: the solutions people come up with are remarkably similar, and the most sustainable solution is discovered less than 10 percent of the time. Moreover, the conditions of the challenge, which are similar to the kinds of constraints under which Mohammed Bah Abba labored, are generally ignored.

The top ten solutions I've received include, in no particular order: (1) a loyalty program that gives you a free rental if your rewind record is clean for a length of time; (2) a small monetary fine of some sort; (3) more rewinders in the store with good signage; (4) splicing reminders into the tape itself; (5) a video case that doesn't allow the tape to be put in if it hasn't been rewound, or modifying the cassette itself so that it won't fit back in the case if it hasn't been rewound; (6) putting the movie on both sides of the tape; (7) cutting the tape to put the ending at the front; (8) eliminating the drop box, monitoring every customer return, and reminding them their tape needs rewinding; (9) enlisting volunteers to rewind the tape in exchange for free rentals; and (10) the all-time favorite—designing a drop box that rewinds the tape when it is inserted.

All of these solutions violate one or more of the limitations I imposed when I presented the problem, however. In other words, it appears to be easier, or at least more common, to think "outside the box" than inside it.

* * *

The first thing I observe when I watch people wrestle with this problem is the almost immediate leap to the solution itself. In an almost reflex action, they begin brainstorming. Unfortunately, leaping to solutions in an instinctive way or intuitive way almost never leads to an elegant solution to a complex problem, because deeper, hidden causes don't get addressed. Jeffrey Schwartz, whom you met in chapter 3, helped me understand this natural, instinctive bias for action: the pattern-making ability of our brain, unless we make a conscious effort to stop it, will take the shortest mental cut to the answer. There's a good reason why this is effective more often than not: most of the problems we face each day simply don't require much more than a quick work-around. By the time we're ready to start our day's work, we probably have already solved a multitude of routine problems: what time to get up, what to wear, how to avoid traffic, and will it be a tall, grande, or venti at Starbucks today? We wouldn't get much accomplished if we had to think deeply about every minor challenge. We need effective shortcuts, not enduring, elegant solutions.

But this natural, more intuitive shortcutting ability can lead us astray. Former CIA analyst Morgan Jones uses the example below to demonstrate how our bias for action can interfere with our efforts to solve problems. Name the individual described here:

A new chief executive, one of the youngest in his nation's history, is being sworn into office on a bleak, cold, cloudy day in January. The new chief executive was raised as a Catholic. He rose to his new position in part because of his vibrant charisma. He is revered by the people and will play a crucial role in a military crisis that will face his nation. His name will become legendary.

I have given this description in lectures and classes to thousands of people, asking the audience to raise their hand when they know who it is, and the vast majority raise their hands before I've uttered the third sentence, concluding that it is John F. Kennedy. But, given this description, I could also be referring to Adolf Hitler. When this description is given to a European audience, they answer Adolf Hitler far more often. So what is going on here? In rather nonneuroscientific terms, as soon as our brain recognizes a piece of information as being part of a preexisting pattern, we leap, subconsciously jumping ahead to a plausible and probable conclusion, instinctively abbreviating our thinking. The pattern called up by our brain works as a kind of mental filter, screening in any information that supports our conclusion, screening out any information that conflicts with it or leads to another possibility. In other words, we don't so much consciously *think* as much as *react*.

This behavior is a version of the brain's "filling in." The upshot of it is we don't get to deeper thinking until we run out of filling-in actions. For example, the next time you sit down to watch television, you'll naturally aim the remote control at the box. You don't need to think about it, because the pattern branded in your brain from the countless times you've taken this action eliminates the need to do so. What happens when the television doesn't come on when you press the power button on your remote? Most of us keep hitting the power button repeatedly, aiming the remote at every possible angle, until we're absolutely certain it won't work. Then a new pattern kicks in: focus on the batteries. So we open up the back—not to replace them, mind you, but roll them around. Only if that still doesn't work do we begrudgingly rise off the couch and replace the batteries. And if that doesn't work, we're stymied. But that's when our real thinking begins.

What does all this have to do with the challenge of the video store? First, the bias for action likely led you to spend nearly all your time listing "top of mind" ideas, and little time thinking about why the rewind problem exists in the first place. It also may have led you to downplay or ignore the importance of the four conditions in framing the problem. This is natural, because it is easier and requires less mental effort than laboring under limits. How much time did you spend thinking about *why* people don't rewind their tape? After years of observing people trying to solve the problem, I can assure you that very few people even raise the question. Most people settle on a solution first, and then try to manipulate it to fit the conditions.

The second point is that a bias for action naturally leads us to want to *do* something. This tendency results in a number of related thinking traps that result in *adding* something to the equation. For example, many of the top ten solutions that arise are really just a version of what hasn't worked in the past: incentives, penalties, reminders, and rewinders. The impulse to *do* leads us to focus on execution, and as a result we ignore the facts, deciding in effect that "they didn't do it right." The outcome is simply another version of what has already been done. The next time you're in the lobby waiting for the elevator to go up to your office or hotel room, count how many people hit the up button even though they can see that you've already pushed it. In analyzing the video rewind problem, a "stop-doing" approach would dictate that we ask ourselves why incentives, penalties, reminders, and rewinders didn't work. How much time did you spend on that question? If it doesn't get asked and answered, we tend to glom on to a solution that is obvious but less than optimal, because it gets us part of the way there and it gives us something to work with. Inevitably, we end up with an unsustainable solution that adds cost and complexity. In looking at the list of most common video rewind solutions, notice that many require the addition of technology not in existence, which not only violates the conditions of the challenge, but is completely unrealistic. In the interest of acting and doing, we can inadvertently "leave out" the most critical facts, which will block the discovery of a more elegant solution. This, paradoxically, is the mirror opposite of the "filling in" effect. Closely related to this is the tendency to simply downgrade the requirement of 100 percent customer rewind, claiming it is impossible. Naturally, we then offer up a reduced objective—getting more or most people to rewind—and declare victory. But as anyone familiar with American football will tell you, the goal is not to reach the 97-yard line. These are the pitfalls of an addiction to addition.

The third and final point is that the filling in that your brain did most likely resulted in your making an assumption—that the videotape must come back to the store rewound. The challenge never stated that the videotape needed to be rewound *before* being returned. But your brain likely filled that in for you, based on the patterns developed through your experience in renting videotapes. The problem simply required the tape to be rewound. The issue of when the tape was to be rewound was never stipulated. This is an example of how *acting*—leaping and filling in—can get in the way of elegance. By spending more time thinking about the deeper cause of the problem, we are often better able to frame the issue without making unwarranted assumptions (which, if you think about it, is an additive action). The true root cause of the problem of unrewound tapes is that a third of the customers are simply lazy and willing to pass their responsibility on to others. Once you understand that, you can see why previous solutions didn't work: nothing at such a low transaction level of a few dollars is going to change a basically lazy person into an accountable one. But you don't need to. So the real issue revolves around *making it impossible not to rewind the tape.* And to do so with little or no cost and without placing additional burden on the customer.

Star Video's solution? Simply let the tapes be rented out unrewound. They simply put a small sticker on the video case, stating, in effect, that the tape may have to be rewound before watching. The solution places no additional burden on the customer—one rewind was all that was ever required—and that hasn't changed. What has changed is where and when the rewind occurs. If you get a tape that hasn't been rewound, you rewind it before watching. But then you're done. The stickers were very inexpensive, and there is no ongoing burden on the store. Problem solved. It's a very simple, sustainable solution, requiring less energy in the form of policing, and less cost in terms of enforcement.

Star Video never had to rewind another tape again. Their customers were fine with the policy change; because they no longer expected a rewound tape, they were not dissatisfied when they didn't get one. They learned to hit rewind first, then get their microwave popcorn and drink, and finally come back to enjoy the show.

Eventually, of course, autorewind VCRs and DVDs made the entire issue irrelevant. But the thinking required to craft a sustainable solution by framing a challenging problem within clear limitations is exactly what we need to realize elegance in our own pursuits, for the simple reason that most of the challenges we face are far more complex than simply getting someone to rewind a tape.

*c.*

The solution to the video rewind challenge is not unlike the "stop doing" approach taken, for example, in the shared space design of the Laweiplein intersection. In both cases, existing controls have been removed, replaced with a "do nothing" approach that offers a far more sustainable way to organize and operate. But what the video challenge demonstrates is that we face two major obstacles in trying to solve problems elegantly. The first is *acting.* The second is *adding.* As the previous discussion showed, all of the typical solutions can be attributed to one or both of these. Moreover, even when clear constraints are offered in an attempt to direct the effort toward a sustainable end, the tendency to act and add can override our better thinking.

In 1957, economics Nobel Laureate Herbert Simon published a book called *Models of Man.* In it, he examined the default human decision-making process in which we tend to go with the first option that offers an acceptable payoff. Simon said that by nature we "satisfice"—his term, combining *satisfy* and *suffice.* In other words, we have a tendency to settle for "good enough," opting for whatever seems to expeditiously meet the minimum requirement needed to move us closer to achieving a given goal. We then stop looking for other ways, including the *best* way, to solve the problem. We rationalize that the optimal solution is too difficult, not worth the effort involved, or simply unnecessary. The instinct to satisfice, though, results in acting and adding, and works against the pursuit of elegance.

To illustrate how satisficing works, and what the remedy might be, take a look at the incorrect Roman-numeral equation below. Imagine that the numbers are sticks. Leaving the plus and equals signs where they are, what is the least number of sticks you need to move to turn the equation into a correct one?

$$XI + I = X$$

Most people get to the answer of "one" almost immediately. They jump in and start moving things around right away, seeing $X + I = XI$ or $IX + I = X$ as good answers, and stop at that point. But these are satisficing answers, and only "good enough." If you stop and think for a moment about the optimal answer to the question of "least number of sticks moved," you realize that the answer ideally would be "zero." Is that possible? Yes. Turn the book upside down for a moment. You don't need to move a single stick. The elegant solution is achievable if you stop for a moment, think about the question a bit more deeply, look at the problem from another perspective, and aim for the ideal. This, though, is the opposite of satisficing.

What does this have to do with sustainable solutions? When we satisfice, we ignore the constraints that carry the paradoxical power to open up new and different ways of looking at things. We mistakenly pose the question "What should we do?" before asking "What is possible?" We want a solution, but we don't have the patience to wait for the optimal one, favoring implementation over incubation. We throw some resources at the problem and move on, or tweak a previous solution and fit it to the current situation. We fail to look more holistically at the challenge. The result is that we simply don't see the best, most elegant solution. It's as MIT lecturer Peter Senge says: "Human endeavors are systems . . . we tend to focus on snapshots of isolated parts of the system, and wonder why our deepest problems never get solved."

In the early 1990s, Peter Senge and Harvard University's Chris Argyris set out to address this issue, focusing on what they eventually called "mental models," a term for the mindset that makes up our own particular perspective or worldview. Argyris went so far as to say that many of our mental models are flawed, because most of what guides our actions is related to one of four intentions: to remain in control, to maximize winning and minimize losing, to suppress negative feelings, and to be as rational as possible. He believed people act this way in order to avoid threat or embarrassment—in other words, most people practice defensive reasoning. Argyris claims that one's mental model plays out in a repetitive pattern he calls the "ladder of inference." It works like this: You experience something, and that becomes the ladder's first rung. You apply your own theory to the situation, and that's the second rung. Next come the assumptions you make, the conclusions you draw, and the beliefs you hold. Finally, you act. But as you climb the ladder, you are becoming more and more abstract in your thought, further from the facts of the situation. And so you are vulnerable to less than optimal action. Because the process feeds back on itself, it strengthens the patterns in your mind, so the next time you're faced with a new situation, you're handicapped from the start. This contributes to the danger of our leaping to solutions as discussed earlier.

Why are we so susceptible to our mind-set? Philosopher Immanuel Kant maintained that the mind is not built to give us raw knowledge of the world; we must always approach it from a special point of view, with a certain bias, to make it meaningful. The implication of this is that because mind-sets represent our own unique view of the world, we instinctively rely on them to help us make sense of it. But these mind-sets are hidden, hard to identify, and we defend them subconsciously. In other words, we tend to *see* only what we *believe*.

Dr. Ian Mitroff, who established the University of Southern California's Center for Crisis Management to analyze human-caused crises, believes that at both the individual and group levels, unmanaged mind-set can be devastating. Mitroff attributes General Motors' dramatic loss of market share in the 1980s at the hands of import car companies to a decades-old, multilevel, flawed mental model: styling and status is more important than quality, foreign cars are no threat, and workers don't make a difference. General Motors only became aware of their faulty thinking when it was far too late.

As a practical matter, more and more people working in jobs today rely on a deep level of knowledge in a special area—what we call *subject matter expertise*—for their livelihoods. But that kind of special knowledge can actually get in the way when it comes to crafting elegant solutions. Special subject matter expertise is really the mother of all mind-sets, the enemy of objectivity. As psychologist Abraham Maslow once said, "If all you have is a hammer, everything looks like a nail." One of my favorite Dilbert cartoon strips depicts a meeting in which a problem is presented, and each attendee around the table suggests a solution that just happens to match their personal "hammer." In the final panel, a porcupine sitting at the end of the meeting table declares, "We must stick them with quills! It's the only way!!"

But how can knowledge be bad? Aren't the experts in a given area the ones who are supposed to have all the sophisticated solutions? Well, let's take a look at how that can play out. Suppose that Janet has been the top sales performer in your company for five years. Her success is due to her deep knowledge of the software system your firm makes and sells. But now all of a sudden Janet has a problem with a major customer. They're threatening to terminate the relationship due to Janet's insistence on using your system as a blanket solution to all their problems. The customer has repeatedly tested some of the software, but hasn't been happy with results. They're complaining that Janet positions herself as an objective problem solver, when in fact she is pushing your software when other programs are more appropriate. Clearly, Janet's knowledge—her biased perspective—has led her to success in your company. On the other hand, that mind-set can endanger your firm's results and reputation going forward.

Dr. Stellan Ohlsson, a psychology professor at the University of Illinois in Chicago, thinks that deep but narrow bands of knowledge can leave us blind to other options. If we base our approach solely on what we know, without widening our perspective, we will inevitably come up short. According to Ohlsson, when we're faced with a problem or challenge, we tend to view it through the lens of our special knowledge and create a mental image of it based on that. But that can block our ability to see the problem in a new or different way and prevent us from considering other alternatives. We go round and round the problem, locked into our old ways of thinking, getting nowhere, until we finally reach a creative stalemate.

In studies of brainstorming sessions, this impasse is reached in under twenty minutes on average. At that point, all of the immediate, top-of-mind ideas have been exhausted, and rather than holding the creative tension, taking a break, and returning to the problem later, most teams simply pick what they consider the best idea proposed and go with it. This is exactly why, contrary to conventional wisdom, simple, unfocused, or open brainstorming lacking optimal time and proper tools is probably not the best way to arrive at insightful solutions. Unless there is a great diversity of knowledge and widely divergent experience in the room, you may fall victim to the limitations of the homogeneity of the group and produce ideas that are nothing more than updated versions of older thinking.

In 1998, Jennifer Wiley conducted an interesting experiment at the University of Pittsburgh designed to point out how knowledge can get in the way of creative thinking. Wiley took a group of baseball experts and a group with no special knowledge of the game. She gave both groups three words: *plate, rest,* and *broken.* The goal was to find a common word that linked all three ideas together. Wiley was targeting the word *home,* and indeed the baseball experts came up with *home plate,* a baseball term, along with *rest home,* and *broken home* a bit quicker than the nonexperts. But then, in a second test, she changed one word in the trio, producing *plate, shot,* and *broken.* She was targeting the word *glass,* as in *plate glass, shot glass,* and *broken glass.* The baseball experts didn't do nearly as well as the nonexperts. Wiley believed that their knowledge of baseball caused them to lock on to *home plate*, and made it much harder to break free of the concept.

You may recognize this as what you experienced with the letter *E* at the beginning of the book. Before I gave you the missing knowledge that enabled you to see the *E* quickly, you undoubtedly looked at the lines in a number of ways and perhaps from a number of different angles, looking for a meaningful pattern. As soon as you saw the *E*, it became difficult to "unsee" it. It's what happened in the videotape rewind challenge—your knowledge derived from your experience renting videos made it more difficult to break free of thinking the tape needed to come back to the store rewound.

Does this mean that the person with the least knowledge about the problem is the person most likely to solve it? No, that's not the case either. It was physicist Albert Einstein who discovered relativity, not Mae West. And while Mohammed Bah Abbah was not an expert in thermodynamics, it was his intimate knowledge of the context surrounding the food decay problem in Nigeria that helped him devise his pot-in-pot desert cooler. Relevant knowledge *is* required. On the one hand, it allows us to think productively, knowledgeably, and logically. On the other hand, it is important to recognize that focusing only on what we already know can limit our ability to think more expansively.

How do we then move beyond the limitations of our mindset to improve that ability? Is there something that offers a useful way to neutralize the dual dangers of acting and adding in our effort to come up with an elegant solution? The short answer is yes. In the words of Ben Hamilton-Baillie, the shared-space designer we met in our exploration of symmetry: "What's wrong with how we engineer things is that most of what we accept as the proper order of things is based on assumptions, not observations. If we observed first, designed second, we wouldn't need most of the things we build."

But it is not quite as simple as the trite cliché "look before you leap." What Ben Hamilton-Baillie really means is that we should become better detectives.

d.

When William J. Bratton was sworn in as the fifty-fourth chief of police for Los Angeles, California, on Monday, October 29, 2002, he immediately began fixing broken windows. He had risen to notoriety as the nation's "top cop," responsible in good part for the rapid and dramatic drop in crime in New York City during the mid-1990s, by implementing a strategy based on what is now widely known as the "Broken Windows" theory.

"Broken Windows" is the title of an article by two public policy scholars, James Q. Wilson and George L. Kelling, that appeared in the March 1982 issue of the *Atlantic Monthly*. Later, in 1996, Kelling and Catherine Coles, an anthropologist and attorney, published a book called *Fixing Broken Windows*. Malcolm Gladwell, a journalist for the *New Yorker*, highlighted the theory in his 2001 book *The Tipping Point*. The essence of the theory centers on minor, "quality-of-life" crimes such as vandalism, litter, graffiti, panhandling, and, of course, broken windows. In the article, Wilson and Kelling use the latter example to propose their theory: "Consider a building with a few broken windows. If the windows are not repaired, the tendency is for vandals to break a few more windows. Eventually, they may even break into the building, and if it's unoccupied, perhaps become squatters or light fires inside." What Wilson and Kelling argued was that these lesser crimes are actually very important, because gone unaddressed they send the message that no one cares, that you can get away with anything. Before long the bad guys run the show, and the community falls into decline as the residents barricade themselves in their homes or flee the neighborhood. The best way to prevent that from happening, the theory claims, is to pay close attention to the smaller, "victimless" crimes, and take care of them right away.

When William Bratton took over in 1990 as head of the New York Transit Police, it was Kelling who helped Bratton implement a zero tolerance for the kinds of subway crimes that previously had been largely ignored: turnstile jumping, panhandling, pickpocketing, and drug dealing. It turned out that a good number of turnstile jumpers and panhandlers had warrants out for their arrests on more serious offenses.

Just before he became mayor of New York City in 1994, Rudy Giuliani attended an all-day seminar on "Broken Windows" policing methods at a think tank called the Manhattan Institute, where George Kelling was a fellow. As mayor, Giuliani hired Bratton as chief of police, and a more far-reaching effort to shut down small crimes in New York City began. Manhattan's infamous "squeegee men"—petty perpetrators of forced vehicle windshield cleaning, followed by demands for money—were tossed in jail. Drug dealers were frisked and arrested for carrying guns. Graffiti was cleaned up, broken windows fixed, litter removed, and the petty criminals dwindled in ranks as they became the center of police attention. Day by day, month by month, block by block, neighborhood by neighborhood, the number of arrests for smaller crimes rose. As they did, the rates of the more serious crimes dropped, quickly and sharply. A new vitality took hold. Before the Giuliani/Bratton campaign, 125th Street in Harlem didn't have a supermarket or a movie theater. Today you'll find Magic Johnson Theaters, Pathmark, The Gap, Barnes & Noble, Disney Store, and the office of former U.S. president William J. Clinton.

The strategy brought to bear all the elements of elegance. Bratton's computer-assisted crime analysis program Comp-Stat showed that a given street or bundle of streets displayed arrest trends similar to those of larger blocks and neighborhoods. This self-similarity could be found all the way up to greater borough and city patterns. In other words, crime rates fell in accordance with what we discovered about fractal symmetry. The essentially subtractive effort seduced the community: the suddenly missing graffiti, lack of broken windows, and absence of unsavory characters attracted people who began to view previously undesirable neighborhoods as inviting and began reoccupying once-vacant buildings. Rather than concoct a grand strategy requiring vast resources, Bratton waged a much more efficient war by viewing an existing asset—a strong but greatly outnumbered police force—as a finite resource and redirecting it to focus on efforts yielding greater impact, without undermining the overall effectiveness of the NYPD. The resourcefulness of the strategy made it sustainable.

As chief of the LAPD, Bratton had every intention of replicating his New York City success, which in fact he is doing. His first move was to pull L.A.'s far smaller police force away from their desks and put them out on the streets. The primary Broken Windows effort is focused on defending public space, a strategy referred to as "community policing." It was to be Bratton's tactic for tackling the biggest problem facing Los Angeles: gangs. He focused community policing on three key, highly deteriorated areas: Skid Row, near downtown L.A., also nicknamed the "Nickel" for the numerous cheap flophouses once inhabited by vagrants; MacArthur Park, riddled with drug dealers and illegal immigrants; and Hollywood, which, though undergoing a renewal effort, had been in decline for decades thanks to its many street hustlers.

The idea behind community policing is simple: police officers should be an essential part of the community and walk its streets to better understand its vital signs and dynamics. This brings police officers into greater contact with citizens on an ongoing and routine basis and enables them to immerse themselves in the problems facing the citizens they have sworn to protect and serve. The problem-solving discipline behind community policing is called SARA, an acronym that stands for scan, analyze, respond, assess. It is an iterative problem-solving cycle. What makes SARA work for the LAPD is the emphasis on *observation*—the scan, analyze, and assess phases are all centered on observation. With observation as the dominant part of the cycle, the action phase of respond becomes much more surgical and precise, so that more can be accomplished with, and for, less. Fighting crime is more sustainable under SARA. In other words, *observation* is LAPD's antidote to *acting* and *adding*.

In March 2007, I was introduced to William Bratton by one of his close advisors, Deputy Chief Mark Perez. Perez is commander of LAPD's Professional Standards Bureau, a 300-person unit that I had been working with closely for several months in partnership on a knowledge-sharing project between LAPD and Toyota. During the project I had gained a better understanding of a number of police methods and gotten an inside look at jail operations, booking procedures, detective work, narcotics investigations, internal affairs, confidential informant handling, and even the elite bomb squad. I had gone on ride-alongs, flown on helicopter missions, and been trained on the use of a firearm.

When I met Chief Bratton at Parker Center in downtown Los Angeles, I was struck by how similar his core philosophy is to that of the engineers and executives of Toyota: they both believe that the job, any job, simply cannot be done in an office, from behind a desk, drawing conclusions and making decisions solely on the basis of reading reports. They both believe in taking a visual approach to solving problems. Had Bratton relied purely on statistics to help craft a strategy in New York City, he would have never focused attention on subways, for the data showed that only 3 percent of the city's major crimes were committed in the subway. He would have been oblivious to the experience of New York City subway riders, who feared for their safety. I got the sense from Bratton that he'd be at every murder scene in person if he could. In his early days on the job in L.A., no matter where Bratton went or what he was doing, he had his adjutant traveling with him at all times relaying the details of every murder investigation as it occurred: He never waited for the written report. He preferred to get the information in real time by cell phone from the investigators on the ground at the crime scene.

Toyota employees know that fact-based problem solving and visual management is at the heart of every decision and that true knowledge comes from clear, accurate, firsthand observation—of customers, of operations, of products. Both Toyota and William Bratton would agree with the wisdom of Sir Arthur Conan Doyle's famed detective, Sherlock Holmes, who, when asked by sidekick Dr. Watson whether he had formed a theory shortly after arriving at the scene of the crime, said: "It is a capital mistake to theorize before one has the facts. Insensibly one begins to twist facts to suit theories instead of theories to suit facts." Similarly, at Toyota, marketing reports and focus groups are all well and good, but those are just data, and while data may *indicate* the facts, there is no substitute for being in the field to gain true insight into problems facing customers and employees. Likewise, if you're a copper in Bratton's rank-and-file, you know that you need to be on top of what's going on no matter what your beat, and the only way to do that is to be out there not just looking, but *seeing.*

In the large situation room reserved for LAPD CompStat meetings, there's a sign with three simple questions that provide the weekly meeting agenda: *Who are they? Where are they? Have they been arrested?* Area commanders are on the hot seat as Bratton's deputies press for answers. These sessions serve both to build accountability and to teach. Field commanders are reminded of the critical importance of carefully listening to and thoroughly questioning all suspects about what they know, not just about the immediate offense, but also about other investigations and unsolved crimes. The process of interrogation and crime scene investigation, and of police detective work in general, is as much of an art as it is a science—quite literally, in fact. As it turns out, art is an observational training tool for the New York Police Department.

If you happened to mistakenly wander into New York's Frick Collection on East Seventieth Street on a Monday, when the art museum—housed in the mansion built by steel industrialist Henry Clay Frick—is closed, you might run into a group of ten to fifteen NYPD officers gazing at the last painting Frick bought before his death in 1919: Johannes Vermeer's *Mistress and Maid*, circa 1667. The painting shows a maid handing a letter to a woman seated at a small writing table in a rather dark and shadowy setting. The woman gazes at the outstretched hand of the maid offering the letter and holds her hand to her chin. Interestingly, in light of what we have learned about *non finito*, the Frick Collection describes the painting this way: "The subject of writing and receiving letters, which recurs frequently in Vermeer's work, is given an exceptional sense of dramatic tension in this painting of two women arrested in some moment of mysterious crisis. The lack of final modeling in the mistress' head and figure and the relatively plain background indicate that this late work by Vermeer was left unfinished."

But the NYPD is not there to appreciate the art, nor are the officers taking a crash course on catching art thieves. They're there to improve their power of observation and hone their visual skills by participating in a program developed by a former educational director for the Frick, geared toward newly promoted officers, sergeants and above. According to NYPD Assistant Chief Diana Pizzuti, "In New York, the extraordinary is so ordinary to us, so in training we're always looking to become even more aware as observers." The officers are given a limited amount of time to arrive at the who, what, where, why, and when of the Vermeer painting. One captain observes that the mistress is right-handed, well-to-do, and that it appears she has dropped her pen. He's not sure about the maid, though, and asks his fellow officers whether she is smirking—and do they detect a defensive posture? As the group moves on to assess works such as

El Greco's *The Purification of the Temple* and William Hogarth's *Miss Mary Edwards,* they learn to scan and analyze an entire canvas quickly but thoroughly. The process is one first of observation and description, moving from foreground to background, followed by analysis and conclusion. Expanding the circle of observation this way can help in analyzing a crime scene. One captain tells the story of a fleeing suspect who fell to the pavement while racing across rooftops to avoid capture. Frick training prompted the officer to stop, take in the entire scene, and widen his search perimeter beyond just the site of impact; he located an automobile on which detectives found palm prints that aided in reconstructing and mapping the intended escape route.

Toyota executives, like William Bratton, swear by the power of thorough observation, so much so that it is a formal guiding principle and practiced at every level of the company. The goal is to build skill in viewing problems and challenges from different perspectives, much like artists, sculptors, and photographers do when they look at their subject from every possible angle to enhance their ability to render "the truth." The Japanese term for this is *genchi genbutsu,* which roughly translated means "go look and see." Interestingly, Toyota designers and engineers often act as undercover detectives when researching and developing a new vehicle. Where undercover detectives insinuate themselves into the lives of criminals under investigation to gain their trust and learn the facts, designers at Toyota will adopt the lifestyle of potential customers to do the same. To prepare for the creation of the very first Lexus in the mid-1980s, the design team lived the life of a luxury car buyer. They leased a beachfront house in Laguna Beach, California, for several months and spent their time shopping in Beverly Hills, golfing in Bel Air, eating at posh restaurants, and visiting trendy nightclubs. They drove around in Mercedeses, BMWs, Cadillacs, Porsches, and Jaguars. They observed valets, caddies, chauffeurs, and caterers serving the wealthy. They conducted similar tours in other large U.S. cities. The luxury scene was foreign to the team, because at that time in Japan only criminals lived in such a way. Their conclusion from this close observation was that luxury automotive customers sought *perfection* in their purchases and possessions.

Similarly, in the early part of the new millennium, having failed to market the Toyota brand to the younger Generation Y, Toyota marketers attended raves, urban art shows, and extreme sporting events in an effort to learn the tastes and preferences of the so-called "new millennials." Toyota came to realize that this group of customers, replete with their tattoos and piercings and to whom they must successfully sell in order to survive the future, sought above all *personal expression* in their possessions, preferring to discover on their own, without being advertised to, products that allowed tailoring and customization. Toyota's new youth brand, Scion, a small, spare, and easily customized series of three vehicles, quickly became the company's fastest-selling brand after it launched in 2003. The cars averaged $15,000, but the young buyers were spending that much again to install carbon fiber trim, flat panel televisions, and high-fidelity sound systems. In an unprecedented move, Toyota eliminated advertising for the brand, choosing instead to place the cars where they could be observed and discovered by potential buyers.

In the factory, a new associate in a Toyota plant is sometimes asked to observe a particular operation while standing within a circle drawn on the floor, known as an "Ohno circle," named for the engineering pioneer Taiichi Ohno. Ohno often would draw a circle on the floor in the middle of a bottleneck area and make a line employee stand in that circle all day to watch the process, directing them to observe and ask *Why?* over and over. Ohno believed that new thoughts and better ideas do not come out of the blue, they come from a true understanding of the process. Typically what happens during this exercise is that you quickly become familiar with the process, and start to see problems, gaps. Because you can't move or take action, you start to ask *Why is this occurring?* Finally, you come to understand the root cause. Then, and only then, can you offer a solution. When the person would report to Ohno any observations made, problems discovered, and solutions recommended—as well as the rationale for them—Ohno would just look at the person and say, "Is that so?"

By requiring keen observation before action, by demanding that one look beyond the obvious surface symptoms to better *see* the deeper causes, by never giving answers and only asking questions, Ohno taught people to stop and think.

*e.*

On a weekend fishing expedition to Transky, on the east coast of South Africa known as the Wild Coast, advertising executive Trevor Field observes a number of women standing next to a windmill, waiting for the wind to blow. Curious, he investigates the situation to discover that the concrete reservoir at the bottom of the windmill is cracked, so it will not hold water. When he passes by the windmill two days later, the women are still there waiting. The troubling scene stays with him.

He discovers how serious the world's water problem is: that over one billion people do not have access to clean water, that water-related illnesses are the single largest cause of disease worldwide, and that nearly 6,000 people each day die due to water-related disease. Moreover, abundant safe water is a little more than a hundred feet below the surface, but the resources do not exist to extract, store, and purify it.

At the same time, Ronnie Stuiver, who drills boreholes for wells in remote areas of South Africa, is bothered by another observation. When he rolls his drilling rig into a village, the children gather to watch him work, fascinated. Without swing sets or playgrounds, their boundless energy has limited outlet. He designs a small-scale model of something he thinks will delight them: a pump with a merry-go-round fitted on top that can be powered by play. As the children spin the merry-go-round, water is pumped from deep in the ground. He puts his prototype on display at an agricultural fair in Johannesburg.

On that particular day, Trevor Field is attending the fair with his father-in-law. He spies Stuiver's pump and instantly sees it not just as a merry-go-round that pumps water, but as a cleverly sustainable way to help people like the women he saw waiting for the wind. He envisions a self-contained, self-sustaining water system, complete with a high-capacity water tank with four large spaces for billboard advertising and public service messages—the revenue from which will pay for maintenance—all powered by children's play. He licenses the idea from Stuiver and forms PlayPumps International to allow the systems to be donated to communities and schools in rural Africa. Today, over 1,000 PlayPumps have been installed in the sub-Sahara, with commitments for 4,000 by 2010.

Elegance is not a matter of superior intelligence. And while the ability to solve problems elegantly does not require the genius of Albert Einstein or Leonardo da Vinci, it does require the scientist's diligence and obsessive attention to detail, coupled with the artist's ingenuity in pursuing possibilities within the clear confines of a chosen medium— the painter's canvas edge, the sculptor's block of marble, the composer's octave, or the writer's alphabet. The awareness of this requirement is growing, and as Richard Florida, author of *The Rise of the Creative Class*, states, "Millions of people are beginning to work and live the way creative people like artists and scientists always have." A sustainable idea is the visible outcome of viewing finite resources as scarce and precious—an opportunity to think anew—and exploiting the one eternal source of creativity and innovation: *observation.*

Keen observation is at the heart of the stories of elegance we have explored: of physicist Richard Taylor's discovery of the fractal nature of Pollock's paintings and the safe ambiguity of Laweiplein, of Leonardo da Vinci's seductive *sfumato* technique and Jean-François Zobrist's hands-off management style, and of Mohammed Bah Abba's desert cooler and William Bratton's microcrime-fighting methods.

It seems that if we can stop, look, and think long enough to ask the right questions and fight our natural tendency to arrive at an immediate answer, we will find ourselves in a better position to see the elegant solution. For many of us, though, it is answers that have consumed our thoughts since we were first-graders. Perhaps it's worth revisiting Rudyard Kipling's poem, "The Elephant's Child":

*I keep six honest serving-men;*
*(They taught me all I knew)*
*Their names are What and Where and When*
*And How and Why and Who.*
*I send them over land and sea,*
*I send east and west;*
*But after they have worked for me,*
*I give them all a rest.*

These are the same six gentlemen I called on in devising the winning line for the *New Yorker* cartoon caption contest.

But there is one last dimension to elegant thinking. As it turns out, even thought is not exempt from a "stop doing" approach. Kipling's last line—*I give them all a rest*—is indeed quite telling, as we shall see.

# *Elegance in Mind*

I AM SITTING IN a comfortable recliner in a darkened room, listening to strange, oddly soothing sounds of some New Age kind of music being played at varying rhythms. There are electrodes wired to my scalp and earlobes. It's the signals being emitted from the goings-on in my head that are responsible for the undulations in the music and their corresponding images on the computer screen before me. A psychedelic screensaver of vivid color and dynamic patterns dances across the monitor: they are, in fact, complex images based on the electrical impulses from brainwaves I'm generating, which have been converted by a mathematical algorithm. I've come to this place, a neurofeedback center in West Los Angeles called BrainPaint, in search of the answer to the question: Is there a way to induce that elusive feeling of being in a state of total creative flow, relaxed focus, and effortless power? In other words, I'm looking for a mindful sense of quiet elegance, the ultimate "stop doing" state of maximum impact with minimum effort.

*a.*

On my first visit with Dr. Jeffrey Schwartz, who I introduced in chapter 3, I was interested in how the brain creates a pattern all on its own, and the corresponding effect when external stimuli interrupt that pattern. The question there was: What gets and keeps our attention in the outside world, and how do these stimuli actually create new patterns in our brain? On this visit, I'm more interested in what happens when *we* are the ones who are consciously or unconsciously initiating an interruption in those patterns—the internal stimuli that can spark new insights.

Through researching how certain notable people have achieved ingeniously elegant solutions, it had become quite apparent that these brilliant flashes of insight had a unique aspect to them. They came at strange times and in random locations. They almost never occurred during the course of a concerted effort focused on solving a problem, but after an intense, prolonged struggle with it, followed by a break. A change of scene and time away seemed to play a part in achieving breakthroughs. I wanted to know why, because it seemed like supporting evidence for a "stop doing" approach, in this case a "stop thinking" approach. Was there any confirmed science behind it?

Most people recognize the *eureka!* moments of legendary insight—Archimedes' discovery of volume displacement occurring during a bath, Einstein's theory of special relativity coming to him in a daydream, and Friedrich von Stradonitz's discovering the round shape of the benzene ring after dreaming of a snake biting its tail. The more you look into how groundbreaking solutions came about, the more you realize how much they share a common element. Philo Farnsworth was plowing a field as a teenager in 1921 when the idea for projecting moving images line by line came to him as he gazed out over the even rows, prompting him to use his knowledge of electrons and vacuum tubes and invent the first electronic television. Richard Feynman was watching someone throw a plate in the air in Cornell University's cafeteria in 1946 when the wobbling plate with its red school medallion spinning around sparked the Nobel Prize–winning idea for quantum electrodynamics. Kary Mullis, another Nobel winner, was driving along a California highway in 1983 when the chemistry behind the polymerase chain reaction (PCR) came to him, stopping him in the middle of the road. In 1995, car designer Irwin Liu sketched the innovative new lines of what became the shape of the first Toyota Prius after helping his child with an elementary school science project involving the manipulation of hard-boiled eggs. Author J. K. Rowling was traveling on a train between Manchester and London in 1990, thinking about the plot of a novel, when the character of Harry Potter flashed in her mind—she was able to work out all the details of a children's story without so much as a pen and paper. Shell Oil engineer Jaap Van Ballegooijen's idea for a snake oil drill came in 2005 as he was watching his son Max turn his bendy straw upside down to better sip around the sides and bottom of his malt glass.

The common element in all of these eureka moments is a quiet mind, severed for a time from the problem at hand. Most artists, musicians, writers, and other creatives instinctively know that the incubation of great ideas involves seemingly unproductive times, but that those downtimes and timeouts are important ingredients of immensely productive, creative periods. Until fairly recently, the how, when, and why of being kissed by the muse was something of a myth and mystery. But now researchers examining how the human brain solves problems can confirm that experiencing a creative insight—that sudden *aha!* flash—hinges on the ability to synthesize connections between seemingly disparate things. And a key factor in achieving that is physical or mental time away from the problem. New studies show that creative revelations tend to come when the mind is engaged in an activity unrelated to the issue at hand. Pressure is not conducive to recombining knowledge in new and different ways, the defining mark of creativity.

At the University of Lübeck in Germany, neuroendocrinologist Ullrich Wagner demonstrated that the ultimate break—*sleep*—actually promotes the likelihood of insights. In one experiment, he gave volunteers some Mensa-style number sequences to solve, along with two logical rules to use in manipulating them to find the pattern. But there was a single, simpler, "hidden" rule that they might discover as they worked through the sequences. The subjects were allowed to practice several times with the given rules and then told to take a break. Some took naps, some didn't. Upon returning to the experiment to continue doing more problems, those who had taken a nap found the hidden rule much more often than those who hadn't. Wagner believes that information is consolidated by a process taking place in the hippocampus— the part of the brain that bundles and repackages memories and fragments of information from other areas and sends them to the frontal cortex to be synthesized into higher-level thought—during sleep, enabling the brain to clear itself and, in effect, reboot, all the while forming new connections and associations. It is this process that is the foundation for creativity. The result is new insight and the *aha!* feeling of the *eureka!* moment.

While no one yet knows what exactly that process is, what is important to know is that putting pressure on ourselves to speed up or artificially influence our brains to work harder, or more intensely, or more quickly, only slows down our ability to arrive at new insights. Ironically, when we let go, when we escape, either physically or mentally, we actually speed up the transformational processes.

But of course, we're reluctant to take those breaks. Aside from the fact that taking a nap at work is generally not considered a good strategy for getting promoted, and that being caught staring off into space can send the message that our current workload is too light, we usually don't design in valuable getaway breaks as a planned, formal part of our problem-solving effort. So why not do so?

Perhaps it's the fear of failure or simply of inaction. Backing off from tackling a complex problem is counterintuitive and goes against our bias for action. It somehow just feels wrong, like preemptive surrender. It's scary to ease up, because we think we may lose our momentum or abandon hope. We get anxious when the ideas aren't forthcoming, so we begin to doubt our creativity, abilities, and intelligence, fearing that if we take our eye off the problem even for a moment, we may lose the energy we've invested. It would be quite convenient to simply take time off, but the reality of the world we live in makes that ever more difficult.

So if we can't always physically remove ourselves from the problem, can we do so mentally? That's exactly the question I posed to Dr. Jeffrey Schwartz.

*b.*

Jeffrey Schwartz is a practicing neuropsychiatrist specializing in nonpharmaceutical ways to unlock some of the most debilitating kinds of patterns in the brain. He's a widely recognized authority who developed a successful cognitive-behavior therapy at the UCLA School of Medicine for patients suffering from obsessive-compulsive disorder (OCD). In other words, he helps people with what he calls "brainlock," because in OCD patients, connections between parts of their brain get locked together, unable to shift from one thought to the next. Obsessions are intrusive, unwelcome, distressing thoughts and mental images, such as "My hands are filthy." Compulsions are the behaviors OCD sufferers perform in a vain attempt to exorcise the fears and anxieties caused by their obsessions, such as washing their hands until they're raw. I'm interested in Jeff's methods not because I'm specifically curious about OCD, but because if he can help people with that kind of mental rigidity and dysfunction, think what we can do with a brain that isn't all locked up.

In chapter 3, I mentioned the term coined by Adam Smith, the Impartial Spectator. Smith defined "the impartial and well-informed spectator," as the ability to stand outside of yourself and watch "the person within" in action. We each have access to this person, and what Jeff teaches his patients to do is to invoke the Impartial Spectator. The notion of the Impartial Spectator is really no different in principle from the mindful awareness practiced through meditation by Buddhist monks, one of the most studied groups in neuroscientific research.

Under the auspices of the Dalai Lama, researchers like Richard Davidson of the University of Wisconsin, Madison, have, since the 1990s, been studying Tibetan monks living in the hills above Dharamsala to understand how meditation affects brain activity. In the most experienced Buddhist practitioners—those with 10,000 hours or more of meditation behind them, called adepts—electroencephalographs (EEGs) show higher than normal levels of the alpha and gamma brainwaves indicative of the state of focused awareness thought to be associated with the moments of the elusive, insightful aha!

The implication of this research is significant: we can learn to quiet our mind, even when a physical break isn't possible or feasible. High performers in athletic competition know that the line between failure and success is very often drawn on the mental field of play. Those who are mentally tough—relaxed, focused, and in the zone—generally emerge the victors. How very elegant if we can improve our thought process by learning how to "stop thinking."

Mindful awareness is something Jeff Schwartz practices daily, through meditation, and something I asked him to teach me how to do. Like most writers, I imagine, I tend to suffer from chatter brain. If I happen to wake up in the middle of the night, it's nearly impossible for me to turn off my thoughts. Sometimes the ideas are good, but often it's just the same old loop being replayed. I wanted to find a way to eliminate the things that might be getting in the way of genuine focus. What I would learn is just how difficult it is to do nothing.

The instructions for the mindful awareness meditation

conducted by ancient Buddhist priests are straightforward enough. They amount to sitting still, breathing, watching yourself breathe—invoking the Impartial Spectator—and not thinking about anything but observing yourself from *outside* yourself. Easy, right? Here's what Jeff Schwartz told me to do:

> Sit still in a chair, in a quiet room, for twenty minutes, and just watch yourself breathe. Pick a time and a place when you can be reasonably sure no one will interrupt you. Close the door to minimize outer distractions. Sit comfortably in a chair, or cross-legged on the floor, with your hands resting in your lap. You can close your eyes, or you can keep them open but unfocused. Place your attention on the inner rim of your nostrils, where you can feel the subtle movement of air as you breathe in and out. Now, "watch" your breathing go in, go out, go in, go out. Make a mental note for each in-breath and out-breath like this: "breathing in," "breathing out." Or just "in" and "out." Try to be aware of the entire in-breath, from the time it starts to the time it stops. This is the time to make the mental note "breathing in," if that's your choice of note. Don't worry about the exact words, it's the process of observing yourself that's critical. Then try to be aware of the entire out-breath, from the time it starts to the time it stops. This is the time to make the mental note "breathing out." Now, if you suddenly notice that your mind has wandered away from your breathing, just make a mental note of that. For example, "wandering, wandering," or "thinking, thinking," or "imagining, imagining." Then gently bring your attention back to

an in-breath or out-breath, and continue observing and making mental notes of those observations.

Jeff Schwartz performs this routine for an hour every day, without fail. I made it for all of about thirty seconds before my mind started to buzz off to faraway places. "The key to the quiet mind," Jeff says, "is the ability to achieve a stable state of relaxed alertness and awareness. That's true mindfulness. That's what sets the stage for what you want." He tells me that Dr. Mark Jung-Beeman, a cognitive neuroscientist at Northwestern University, has shown that the origins of insight reside in resting-state brain activity. Jung-Beeman and his team wanted to understand the differences in what goes on in the brain between the two different types of problem-solving: the methodical, conscious, analytical search method, and the sudden aha! insight, where the solution pops seemingly from nowhere into our consciousness. Using high-density EEGs to record brainwave activity, Jung-Beeman was able to show that volunteers solving a series of anagrams via the sudden insight method experienced a burst of fast brainwaves known as gamma waves right at the aha! moment. Preceding the gamma waves, however, was a resting state of slower alpha waves, which indicate a relaxed but focused brain activity indicative of the proverbial zone. The Buddhist adepts all showed very high levels of this type of activity.

It is at this point that Jeff asks me if I want to *see* what my own brain is up to. Would I like to see what kind of brainwaves I'm generating? Would I be interested in discovering another way to achieve that state of relaxed awareness? The notion that the quiet mind not only gives rise to being "in the zone" but also sets the table for eureka moments is intriguing. And that's how I wound up in a dark room with electrodes wired to me, testing out BrainPaint.


*c.*


Bill Scott, another neuroscientist working with UCLA, is the founder of BrainPaint. He has developed treatment protocols used by other neurofeedback centers all over the world, some of which cater in secret to executives, Wall Street traders, and professional athletes looking for ways to train the brain to find "the zone." The 2006 World Cup champion Italian soccer team, for example, trained in a secretive European neurofeedback center called the Mind Room. Scott has agreed to give me a few hours of his time to take me through an extended neurofeedback training session.

Anyone who has forgotten their opening line before an audience after countless perfect rehearsals, or who has missed an easy "gimme" putt at a critical moment, or has lost a tennis match by double-faulting the last point or netting a shot they never miss in practice understands what can happen when we don't relax, when we lose our focus and allow our confidence to be eroded by self-doubt. We miss the mark, over or under. We do too much, or not enough. It's never pretty and never elegant. But all of us have experienced just the opposite as well, those times when everything clicks, when our efforts are effort*less*—we're in full flow, reaction times seem quicker, we know we can't miss, we're on, and all our jokes are funny. In sports, it's called playing in the zone. And there's no better way of describing the goal of neurofeedback training: to unconsciously achieve that zone consistently, even in the face of errors, so that whatever we're attempting, there's a higher degree of elegance to our performance. Greater impact, less effort.

"You can't come at this head-on," Bill tells me. "You can't just flip a switch and power your way to the zone. It's just the opposite." I had told him I was an avid cyclist, so he put things in terms I could easily grasp. "When you are riding fast, do you tell your heart to beat faster?" No—just my legs. "And when you are riding fast, do you tell your lungs to breathe deeper in order to take in more oxygen?" No, again. "Most of what your body does to rise to the occasion is not coming from conscious commands, it's coming from the power of your brain, automatically. If you improve the brain's functioning, then you improve your game, whatever your game may be. This really is all about getting out of your own way so you can perform at your best." Okay, that's starting to sound like exactly what this whole book is about.

As he starts hooking me up, Bill explains this type of feedback. EEGs work by detecting electrical signals given by brainwaves, all of which have different wavelengths and frequencies. Neurofeedback works the way most any feedback mechanism works, be it a mirror, a videotape of your performance, an audience: your actions get fed back to you so you can adjust accordingly. In the case of neurofeedback, software converts the electrical signals from your brain through the EEG and gives you visual and audio feedback on your mental and emotional states. You can see and hear, in real time, what's going on between your mind and your brain through the images on the computer screen and the music that's being played, all of which corresponds to the various types of brainwaves you're generating. Your brain then learns to improve the management of these states. Once these new developmental skills are learned, they eventually become automatic, like riding a bike or tying our shoes—no thinking required.

In fact, this feedback training is in principle really no different from the methods used by cycling coach Chris Carmichael. As a cyclist, I wear a heartbeat monitor to make sure I stay within a certain range to achieve various training goals. I'm not directly controlling my heartbeat—I'm doing it indirectly by controlling my exertion level. I know from Carmichael's field tests the exact number of beats my heart must not rise above if I want to sustain maximum power without lactic acid buildup—the chemical process that causes the burning feeling in your muscles when you overload them with exercise. For me, that rate is 172 beats per minute. This is my lactate threshold. If I go beyond that for too long, my legs burn and soon shut down, unable to continue due to lack of oxygen in the muscles. If I have an eight-mile mountain road to ride, and I want to make it to the top as fast as I can, I have to regulate my pedal cadence and gears to make sure my exertion level doesn't rise much above 172 beats per minute.

This is the principle behind neurofeedback training, as well. The underlying philosophy is the same as that behind mindful meditation—indirectly influencing the physical connections in the brain by directing the mind, using a bit of technology as a guide. Here, by training your brain to a resting-state of alpha, you not only set yourself up to more automatically find the zone, but also set the stage for the kind of creative insights that result in the *aha!* moment.

Neurofeedback has its critics, and I was a tad skeptical. Could just being at a neurofeedback center listening to soothing music be enough to put you in the zone? A laboratory study conducted by Tobias Egner and John Gruzelier, faculty of medicine researchers at the Department of Cognitive Neuroscience and Behaviour, Imperial College London, studied the use of neurofeedback protocols on student performances at the Royal College of Music in London. One group of students received training, the other didn't. The goal was to compare performance improvement before and after the training process. The students in both groups were assessed on two musical pieces of about fifteen minutes in length, performed for a Royal Academy audience of faculty members. The performances were videotaped, placed in random order, and evaluated by four different judges not affiliated with the college, who did not know the students and who were blind as to which had received neurofeedback training. Evaluations were made on ten-point scales adapted from a set of standard music performance criteria developed by the academy. The neurofeedback group underwent ten fifteen-minute training sessions over five weeks. Both groups continued to practice their performance pieces. The before and after results were impressive. The group receiving the neurofeedback training showed a 15 percent improvement in overall quality, stylistic accuracy, musical understanding, and interpretative imagination, compared to the group that had received no such training. That group showed no improvement between the two performances. When the experiment was repeated with a different group of students, the results were the same.

The first thing Bill Scott had me do was to play what he calls the Performance Game. It's a game of accuracy and speed. The goal is to help set a personal target level of alpha activity. It's simple enough to play. I have to move a playing card–size image from left to right across the screen to cross the finish line on the right as quickly as I can. Letters on the card randomly flash *L*, *R*, or *P*, which stand for left, right, or pause. In my hand is a computer mouse. I hit the left button when *L* flashes, the right button when *R* flashes, and do nothing when *P* flashes. I have nine minutes to move the card over the finish line. The card advances about a sixteenth of an inch if I hit the right button, and I can go as fast as I want—the game will keep up. If I goof, though, the card retreats a step, so there's a cost to making an error, just like in the real world. It's a very simple game, with a very simple goal—no special talent, knowledge, or skill is required. I'm really competing against myself. I'm the one in control, and I have no opponent whose moves I must compete against. There's no pressure other than what I put on myself. It's not like I have to sink a ten-foot putt in front of two thousand people to win the Masters. How hard can this be? I started off fine . . .

*L-R-L-R-L-L-P-R-R-P-P . . . Piece of cake! So I'll speed it up a bit, push it. Still good. I'll set the record. Go faster. Oops. Mistake. Deep breath. Why'd that happen? Wasn't expecting it. Slow down a bit . . . good, good. Huh? Slipped up. That was dumb. R looked like a P. Shake it off . . . but don't do it again! Faster now, back up to speed. Good, good. We're cruising. Step on it a bit. Aagghh! Idiot. This should not be happening. Again! And again! What's going on here?! What, another? Keep going, going. Again. Stop! Okay, slow now. That's the key, slow it down, Matt, no more mistakes. Go really slow. Just no goofs. Don't think about them. R-P-P-P-L-L-R-P-P. Why so many Ps? Here we go. Good, good. Now we're clicking, error-free. Deep breath, try to relax. Take it easy . . . This is so sim . . . darn! Slight goof. Done!*

I was as focused as I knew how to be, but what distracted me and lowered my performance was, well, *me*—my mistakes and self-talk. Once or twice I clearly told myself to hit a different button than I actually did. As the self-pressure mounted, I fell into a downward spiral of performance that took a great deal of focus to pull out of.

Here's a graph of my performance.

## MATT'S ALPHA RELATED TO ERRORS DURING PERFORMANCE GAME

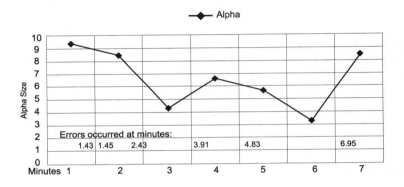

The best way to read this is to note simply that as my errors started occurring, my alpha level dropped dramatically, and where the alpha waves are on the rise is where I tend to be more error-free. But what this initial performance shows is that there may be an ideal alpha wave range for me, where I had the fewest errors. It's important to realize that it's not as simple as "high alpha is better" or "low alpha is better." The goal is to identify a range correlating to my better performance. This simple game, with so little on the line, was so very revealing.

The Performance Game was just part one of my visit. The next step was to go through a full feedback session of around twenty minutes, in which Scott took me through a guided visualization exercise, my eyes alternately open and closed, based on his direction. I was focusing on a mental image of myself as a little boy of about four. I have a picture of me at that age, with a bag of gumdrops in my hand and a rather weathered old teddy bear under my arm, sitting on the curb at the end of the driveway, waiting for my grandpa to visit. Monitoring the brainwave feedback, Bill told me to hold that image in my mind. Explore it deeper. So I imagined what I must have been feeling, how untroubled I must have been. Then he let me watch the patterns on the screen and listen to the music, both of which changed based on brainwaves I was generating. The Brain-Paint software helps train your brain to stay in the zone. Through the feedback from the on-screen images, and attempting to reproduce them by focusing on the mental scenes discovered through the visualization exercises, new patterns get made in your brain. My goal in the future—it takes at least a couple dozen sessions to realize significant results—would be to try to reproduce those cues on-screen by revisiting that image of myself as a little boy. Doing so would help me find that zone of relaxed awareness.

The most fascinating part of the session was how Bill Scott's BrainPaint software converted the signals I was sending. BrainPaint differs from other feedback technologies in a rather significant way. Bill Scott wanted a way to illustrate the complexity of a person's EEG. Before he developed the algorithm for BrainPaint, neurofeedback systems only gave feedback on the linear parts of the EEG—frequency and amplitude. In other words, all you would see was a single wave line displayed on a simple $x$-$y$ axis. "That's like using a triangle to illustrate a mountain," says Bill. "Brainwaves do not travel in straight lines." Sarah Susanka had said something very similar regarding two-dimensional floorplans in determining an appropriate living space.

Bill wanted to provide feedback on *all* the textured information coming from a brainwave. In other words, in addition to describing ocean waves by simply detailing how high they are and how often they crash on the beach—simple linear measurements—he wanted to describe all the various nonlinear nuances a surfer in the water experiences: curvature, speed, cross-currents, undertow, curl, location, volume, water temperature, etc. Moreover, Bill wanted to capture the essential *nature* of the patterns being produced. So he began searching for a better means by which the nonlinear morphology of brainwaves could best be extracted and rendered in real time. There was only one way to do that. Fractals. Those elaborately ordered geometries and richly detailed symmetries that come from chaos, governed by simple and self-repeating rules. Pollock's drips. Nature's fingerprints.

Below you will see an image taken at the time during my BrainPaint session when I was, in effect, able to get out of my own way—when I was in the general vicinity of Jeff Schwartz's "stable state of relaxed awareness." Re-creating this image would become my target in follow-up sessions. Notice that not only is it bilaterally symmetrical, it is fractal—if you look closely at the small parts you will see a self-similar pattern of the whole.

I no longer think this is surprising. Our brains are clearly symmetrical, with a left and right hemisphere. The dendrites and neurons that send messages to and fro across our brain are every bit as fractal as the branches and roots of a tree. Perhaps professor Peter Atkins of Oxford University was on

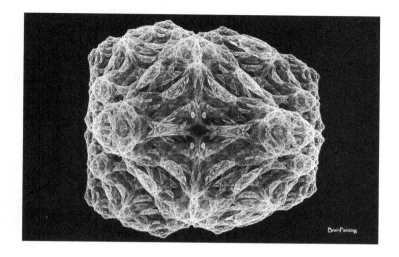

to something when he wrote, "I wonder whether fractal images are not touching the very structure of our brains. Could it be that a fractal image is of such extraordinary richness, it is bound to resonate with our neuronal circuits and stimulate the pleasure I infer we all feel."

And so we have come full circle to the place where we began our pursuit of elegance. It would seem that we all have some Jackson Pollock in us. As I left BrainPaint, it occurred to me that there's a fine line between not thinking enough and thinking too much.

Elegance is all about learning how to walk that line on a more consistent basis.

# Acknowledgments

To BE GRANTED the creative license to indulge my curiosity through a written work tied to a major publisher's balance sheet is, for me, the ultimate privilege. And for that I wish to thank a number of indispensable individuals.

The Broadway team defines true professionalism. My ideas were improved in every possible way by my editor, Roger Scholl, who, in assessing the potential of my original proposal, used the kind superlatives every writer dreams of hearing. I'll never forget that first phone call, and I thank him for his wisdom, and for taking the laws of subtraction to heart in his treatment of the narrative. His former colleague Sarah Rainone offered invaluable guidance as well through the early versions. I'm also grateful for the efforts of the folks who actually put this book in your hands: Michael Palgon, Meredith McGinnis, Nicole Dewey, and Liz Hazelton. Their talents were complemented by the wizardry of my publicist, Barbara Henricks.

Over the course of the last five years I've come to rely heavily on the impeccable judgment of my agent, John Willig. He wears many hats well, as he is at once a sounding board, a creative counsel, a tireless advocate, and at times a much-needed tranquilizer. Without him, my proposal would have never crossed Roger Scholl's desk.

A storyteller is only as good as his subjects, and the difficulties of getting access to the busy people whose stories I've told were greater than I could have imagined. For their generosity in sharing their time with me, I wish to thank them all. Boyd Matson, for teaching me about standing still when hippos charge. Kara Platoni, for allowing me insight into the unreachable and inimitable Donald Knuth. Dr. Richard Taylor, for his complete abundance. Hans Monderman, Martin Cassini, and Ben Hamilton-Baillie, for their collective guided tour through the intriguing world of shared space design. Dr. Jeffrey Schwartz, for indoctrinating me into the disciplines of neuroscience and mindful meditation. Chris Carmichael, for allowing me a peek inside elite athletic training; he has one of the coolest jobs in the world. Jean-François Zobrist, for being patient with someone unworldly enough to speak only English. Sarah Susanka, whose personal elegance and prolific talent I admire openly. George and Debbie Knopfler, for providing the client side of the Susanka experience. Bill Scott, for letting me see what my brain is doing up there.

It is easy to lose sight of the audience in writing a book. My friend Steve Johnson, who reads with an eagle's eye more books than a librarian, performed admirably in the role of chief beta-tester. I relied on him to give me the unvarnished views of a savvy skeptic. I was more than elated to receive his enthusiastic encouragement.

I admire and respect Guy Kawasaki's ability to create a following, so I'm both thankful and lucky to have had him not only digest the book's message, but put it to work in what could be the most elegant foreword ever written.

There was much to do and think about on this journey in search of elegance, and I spent an inordinate amount of time, as they say, "in my head." I was graciously granted the time and space I needed by my wife, Deva, and my daughter, Morgan, who deserve medals for surviving my protracted mental absenteeism. Their patience and support could only come from love.

Any writer would feel fortunate to have received so many generous gifts. I certainly do.

# Notes

PROLOGUE

*The Missing Piece*

1 *nearly twelve million television viewers:* The Associated Press released the
following newswire on June 13, 2007: "Sopranos Whacks Most
Rivals—NEW YORK—The 11.9 million viewers who watched
'The Sopranos' finale brought HBO to the edge of a historic feat:
A show on a pay-cable network available in about 30 million
homes was more popular last week than all but one show in the far
larger world of broadcast television. Only the premiere of NBC's
'America's Got Talent,' with 13 million viewers, did better, Nielsen
Media Research said. ABC, CBS and Fox are all available in 111
million homes for no extra charge, and nothing they aired last week
did better than 'The Sopranos.' It was the fourth-most-watched
episode of 'The Sopranos' since the mob drama premiered on
HBO in 1999, and the most since the 2004 season premiere. With
on-demand services, multiple showings on HBO this week and
DVR recordings, it's unclear how many people will actually watch

the finale. The show topped Game 2 of the NBA Finals (8.6 million viewers) and the Tony Awards (6.2 million) in direct competition Sunday night, Nielsen said."

1 *more than twenty major awards:* The history of *The Sopranos,* including facts about David Chase, the show, awards, and episode guide can be found at http://www.hbo.com/sopranos.

2 "The Sopranos *wasn't only a great show*": Peggy Noonan's Declarations column dedicated to the last episode of *The Sopranos,* entitled "Old Jersey Real—The Greatness of 'The Sopranos,' " appeared on OpinionJournal.com Friday, June 8, 2007, as well as in the print edition of *Wall Street Journal,* June 9, 2007. The column in its entirety can be found at http://opinionjournal.com/columnists/pnoonan.

3 *unparalleled level of postshow scrutiny:* There are two good analyses of the *Sopranos* finale. The first is given by Bob Harris (author of *Prisoner of Trebekistan*) on his June 15, 2007, blog entry at http://BobHarris.com. Over 80,000 people viewed his analysis within forty-eight hours of his post. The second is given by Michael Cavna, TV editor for the Style section of the *Washington Post,* on his June 17, 2007, blog post entitled "Eureka! Solving the Sopranos."

4 *the words of Chinese philosopher Lao Tzu:* Lao Tzu, *Tao Te Ching,* trans. Gia-Fu Feng and Jane English (Vintage Books, 1989), ch. 11.

7 *charging mama hippos:* "How to Stand Still When the Hippos Charge" was the title of Boyd Matson's lecture in a series he and I participated in at Southern Nazarene University in late 2007, and I was able to spend time the following year with Boyd as he explained a variety of similar strategies. Boyd is a longtime adventure journalist for *National Geographic,* past host of the *Explorer* television series, and currently the host of a new National Geographic series airing on PBS called *Wild Chronicles.* You can find out more about Boyd at http://www.nationalgeographic.com/speakers/profile_matson.html.

9 *"stop doing" argument:* Jim Collins's editorial, entitled "Best New Year's Resolution? A 'Stop Doing' List" appeared in the Forum section of *USA Today,* December 30, 2003. You can find the article on www .jimcollins.com, along with a short audio clip on how to "stop doing."

11 *psychologists at the University of Illinois:* The study was conducted by Denise C. Park of the University of Illinois and consisted of showing both young and elderly subjects from the United States and Singapore some two hundred complex scenes while scanning their brains with fMRI. See "The Hidden Power of Culture," in *Scientific American Mind* 18, 4 (August/September 2007), pp. 9–13.

CHAPTER ONE
## Elements of Elegance

13 *ShuttleGirl:* The story of ShuttleGirl was covered by Victoria C. Hallett, staff writer for the *Harvard Crimson,* who wrote two articles on ShuttleGirl: "ShuttleGirl's Identity Revealed" (May 21, 2001) and "The Boys Behind ShuttleGirl" (June 7, 2001).

15 *Randy Nelson:* Jeri Fischer-Krentz, staff writer for the *Charlotte Observer,* wrote a good article on Randy Nelson's course on short prose fiction. See Fischer-Krentz, "He Wants His Short Prose to Challenge," *Charlotte Observer,* December 11, 2005.

15 *six months in 1983:* The story of the Civil Rights Commission was covered in "Civil Rights," *New York Times,* November 12, 1983.

17 *Donald Knuth:* Kara Platoni, a former journalist writing for the *East Bay Express,* was kind enough to allow me full access to her profile piece and story notes of her in-depth interview with the fiercely private Professor Knuth. Platoni, "Love at First Byte," *Stanford Magazine* (May/June 2006).

19 *Euler wrote about a mathematical array:* Leonhard Euler's 1782 article was called "Investigations on a New Type of Magic Square," and can be downloaded at www.math.dartmouth.edu/~euler/docs/ translations/E530.pdf.

21 *Sudoku addiction:* Will Shortz's comments on his addiction to Su-doku can be found in Jessica Bennet, "Will Shortz on the Lure of Sudoku—How the Game Can Help Your Health, Your Brain, and Your Self-Image," *Newsweek* (February 24, 2006).

23 *mental "rush":* Mark A. W. Andrews, professor of physiology and di-rector of the Independent Study pathway at the Lake Erie College of Osteopathic Medicine, writing in the August/September 2007 issue of *Scientific American Mind,* answered the question posed by Kirk McElhearn, of Guillestre, France, in the magazine's "Ask the Brains" section: "Why are games like Sudoku so mentally satisfying? Do they activate a pleasure center in the brain, or do they merely pro-vide the satisfaction of solving problems?"

25 *Zero-Zero-Zero:* Karen Hansen writes about this Mitsubishi program in "A Roller-Coaster Year," *The Pantagraph* (January 18, 2004).

27 *collection of road signs:* Donald Knuth's diary of his diamond-shaped road sign collection can be found at http://www-cs-faculty .stanford.edu/~knuth/index.html.

# CHAPTER TWO

*Desperately Seeking Symmetry*

30 definition *of symmetry:* Three great books on symmetry are Hermann Weyl, *Symmetry* (Princeton Unversity Press, 1952); Mario Livio, *The Equation That Couldn't Be Solved—How Mathematical Genius Discovered the Language of Symmetry* (Simon & Schuster, 2005); and *Why Beauty Is Truth—A History of Symmetry* (Basic Books, 2007). Mario Livio cites Weyl's definition of symmetry as the best as well.

32 *"almost too beautiful to be wrong":* Brian Greene begins his discussion of the aesthetics of symmetry with the story of Einstein's reaction to Dutch physicist Hendrik Lorentz's 1919 congratulatory telegram, in Chapter 7 (pp. 166–83) of *The Elegant Universe—Superstrings, Hidden Dimensions, and the Quest for the Ultimate Theory* (W.W. Norton,

1999). In Greene's view, symmetry is the magic in string theory, and Chapter 7 is entitled "The 'Super' in Superstrings."

34  *"akin to a cosmic symphony":* Greene's description of the universe as being like a cosmic symphony is found in *The Elegant Universe* in Chapter 6, entitled "Nothing But Music: The Essentials of String Theory," the first chapter in Part III: The Cosmic Symphony.

35  *Greene's illustration . . . sequence of letters:* The example of the hidden word is found in *The Elegant Universe,* pp. 300–302, in a section called "The Power of Symmetry."

36  *Taylor is no ordinary physicist:* The discussion of Richard Taylor's work is based on interviews with him in February 2008, while he was on sabbatical in Auckland, New Zealand. The story of Richard Taylor's discovery of the fractal nature of Jackson Pollock's art came to my attention in his *Scientific American* article, "Order in Pollock's Chaos" (December 2002), pp. 116–21. A number of Taylor's articles and links to others can be found at his University of Oregon faculty Web page: http://materialscience.uoregon.edu/taylor/art/info.html.

37  *reenact the story of French painter Yves Klein:* Richard Taylor told the story of Yves Klein in an essay, "Personal Reflections on Pollock's Fractal Paintings," published in a special edition of the *Journal of History, Science & Health* 13 (2006), pp. 108–23.

39  *piqued the nation's ire:* The profile piece on Jackson Pollock appears in *Life* magazine's August 8, 1949, issue.

39  *"Jack the Dripper":* This label comes from another *Life* article on Pollock published in the August 27, 1956, issue.

43  *coined in 1975:* B. B. Mandlebrot's seminal work on fractals is contained in his book, *The Fractal Geometry of Nature* (W.H. Freeman, 1977).

47  *Taylor conducted a study:* The experiment testing the appeal of fractal complexity is described in Richard P. Taylor et al., "Universal Aesthetic of Fractals," *Chaos and Graphics* 27 (2003), p. 813.

53 *22,000 cars:* Details of the before and after statistics of the
Laweiplein design can be found in P. Euser, "The Laweiplein:
Evaluation of the Reconstruction into a Square with Roundabout,"
*Noordelijke Hogeschool Leeuwarden/Verkeerskunde* (March 2006), pp. 5–18.

55 *"Every road tells a story":* Author interview with Hans Monderman,
November 2007, United Kingdom. See also Tom McNichol,
"Roads Gone Wild," *Wired* 12, 12 (December 2004). Available
online at www.wired.com/wired/archive/12.12/trafic.html.

57 *Martin Cassini:* Martin Cassini's work on this subject can be found in
two places: (1) Martin Cassini, "The Case Against Traffic Lights,"
BBC News, January 14, 2008, which you can view by going to
http://news.bbc.co.uk/2/hi/programmes/newsnight/7187165.
stm; and (2) "In Your Car No One Can Hear You Scream! Are
Traffic Controls in Cities a Necessary Evil?" *Institute of Economic
Affairs 2006* (Blackwell Publishing). This article is available on Martin's Web site, at http://www.freewebs.com/mjcassini.

57 *"how traffic controls came about in the first place":* Author interview with
Martin Cassini, February 2007, United Kingdom.

58 *Roger Morrison:* Roger Morrison, "The Comparative Efficiency of
Stop Signs and Stop-and-go Signals at Light-traffic Intersections,"
*Annual Meeting Compendium, Institute of Transportation Engineers* (March
1931), 39–49.

61 *"70 percent of traffic signs":* Author interview with Ben Hamilton-
Baillie, February 2007, United Kingdom. Good articles on home
zones and shared space design include "Shared Space: Reconciling
People, Places and Traffic," *Built Environment* 34, 2 (2008); Emma
Clarke, "The Evolution of Shared Space," *Traffic Engineering &
Control* (September 2006); Ben Hamilton-Baillie, "What Is Shared
Space?" 2006. Available on Ben's Web site at http://www.hamilton-
baillie.co.uk.

65 *apparent chaos:* A number of videos of shared space all over the world
are available on YouTube. Search for "Traffic Monderman"

and "Shared Space." Here are a couple: http://www.youtube .com/watch?v=tye8zjr7pZO and http://www.youtube.com/ watch?v=2IuZ0eQA35c. Many people believe shared space wouldn't work in places like hypertraffic areas such as Cairo and India, due to "culture." Here's a video showing how it works well in India: http://www.youtube.com/watch?v=RjrEQaG5jPM.

66 *the Montana Paradox:* Chad Dornsife of the National Motorists Association wrote two important articles on the Montana Paradox: "Montana: No Speed Limit-Safety Paradox" (February 11, 2000) and "Fatal Accidents Double on Montana's Interstates" (May 10, 2001). Both can be found on the Association's Web site, http://www.motorists.org.

68 *partnered with General Motors:* Paul S. Adler gives a good description of the turnaround by Toyota of the General Motors factory in "Time and Motion Regained," *Harvard Business Review* 71, 1 (1993), pp. 97–108.

68 *Sans . . . Lessness:* Samuel Beckett, "Lessness," *New Statesman* (May 1, 1970).

70 *renowned theater scholar:* Ruby Cohn, *Back to Beckett* (Princeton University Press, 1973).

70 *Elizabeth Drew and Mads Haahr:* Elizabeth Drew and Mads Haahr, "Lessness: Randomness, Consciousness and Meaning," Fourth International CAiiA-STAR Research Conference, Perth, Australia, August 2002.

CHAPTER THREE:
## Seduced by Nothing

73 *"What strikes us first":* E. H. Gombrich, *The Story of Art,* 16th ed. (Phaidon Press 1950, 1995), pp. 300–303.

74 *sfumato:* E. H. Gombrich, "Blurred Images and the Unvarnished Truth," *The British Journal of Aesthetics* 2 (1962), pp. 170–79.

76 *British Romantic period:* Wendelin A. Guentner, "British Aesthetic Discourse, 1780–1830: The Sketch, the Non Finito, and the Imagination," *Art Journal* (Summer 1993).

77 *Paul Cézanne:* Jonah Lehrer, *Proust Was a Neuroscientist* (Houghton Mifflin, 2007), pp. 114–17.

77 *Joe Morgenstern:* See "Morgenstern's Picks: Silence, Loud and Clear," *Wall Street Journal,* January 5–6, 2008.

79 *minimalism, especially relating to buttons:* The two best articles on the iPhone launch and Steve Jobs's button phobia are Paul Kedrosky, "The Jesus Phone," *Wall Street Journal,* June 29, 2007; and Nick Wingfield, "Hide the Button: Steve Jobs Has His Finger on It: Apple CEO Never Liked the Physical Doodads, Not Even on His Shirts," *Wall Street Journal,* July 25, 2007.

82 The Principles of Psychology: William James, *Principles of Psychology* (Holt, 1890), http://psychclassics.yorku.ca/James/Principles.

83 *curiosity-seeking behavior:* Daniel E. Berlyne, *Conflict, Arousal, and Curiosity* (McGraw-Hill, 1960).

84 *extensive analysis of fifty bars:* Leonard Meyer, *Emotion and Meaning in Music* (University of Chicago Press, 1956).

84 *reinterpreted the psychological work:* George Loewenstein, "The Psychology of Curiosity: A Review and Reinterpretation," *Psychological Bulletin* 166 (1994), pp. 75–98.

87 *Dilip Soman and Satya Menon:* Satya Menon and Dilip Soman, "Managing the Power of Curiosity for Effective Web Advertising Strategies," *Journal of Advertising* 31, 3 (Fall 2002).

90 *private practice office of Dr. Jeffrey Schwartz:* My first interview with Jeffrey Schwartz, M.D., was in February 2008, in Los Angeles, California.

91 *the Impartial Spectator:* Adam Smith, *The Theory of Moral Sentiments* (A. Millar, 1759).

93 *Gestalt movement in psychology:* Christian von Ehrenfels, "On Gestalt Qualities," *Psychological Review* 44, 6 (November 1937), pp. 521–24.

93 *blind spot of the eye:* Vilayanur S. Ramachandran and Diane Rogers-Ramachandran, "Mind the Gap: The Brain, Like Nature, Abhors a Vacuum," *Scientific American Mind* (April 2005), p. 100.

95 *it's not just your eyes:* Richard Warren, "Auditory Illusions and Confusion," *Scientific American* 223, 12 (1970), pp. 30–36.

96 *loud sound burst:* Takayuki Sasaki, "Sound Restoration and Temporal Localization of Noise in Speech and Music Sounds," *Tohuku Psychologica Folia* 39 (1980), pp. 79–88.

98 *opinion of chocolate:* The University of Iowa chocolate experiment is found in Dhananjay Nayakankuppam, Baba Shiv, and Himanshu Mishra, "The Blissful Ignorance Effect: Pre Versus Post Action Effects on Outcome-Expectancies Arising from Precise and Vague Information," University of Iowa Health Sciences press release, January 30, 2008. To be published in *Journal of Consumer Research.*

98 *featuring a gorilla:* Aaron O. Patrick, "Big Clients Beat a Path to Fallon in London: Shop Gets Buzz, Billings with Edgy Campaigns; Gorilla-Suit Ad is a Hit," *Wall Street Journal,* December 11, 2007. You can view the ad on YouTube at: http://www.youtube.com/watch?v=TnzFRVILwIo.

99 *satisfaction center in the brain:* A short discussion of the brain's satisfaction center can be found in Mark A. W. Andrews, "Ask the Brains," *Scientific American Mind* (August/September 2007).

100 *link between curiosity and regret:* Eric Dijk and Marcel Zeelenberg, "When Curiosity Killed Regret: Avoiding or Seeking the Unknown in Decision-Making Under Uncertainty," *Journal of Experimental Social Psychology* 43 (2007), pp. 656–62.

102 *cartoon caption contest:* There are two good articles on the history of the *New Yorker* cartoon caption contest: Ben Greenman, "Your Caption Here," *New Yorker,* May 2, 2005; and Ramin Setoodeh, "Behind the Scenes: At the Caption Contest," *Newsweek,* December 11, 2006.

CHAPTER FOUR

*Laws of Subtraction*

106 *In-N-Out Burger:* Two good rundowns on In-N-Out Burger and the secret menu can be found on the following blogs: www.laughingsquid

.com in a June 17, 2007, post by Scott Beale entitled "In-N-Out Burger, a Fast Food Underdog with a Cult Following," and www .badmouth.net in a February 24, 2005, post by John Marcotte entitled "In-N-Out's Secret Menu."

108 100x100: The 100x100 story in bite-by-bite, photographic detail can be found on the January 23, 2006, entry of http://whatupwilly .blogspot.com, entitled "In-N-Out 100x100."

109 *as mystified as customers:* Tom McNichol, "The Secret Behind a Burger Cult," *New York Times,* August 14, 2002.

110 *no stranger to cycling:* The story of Chris Carmichael and Lance Armstrong is based on my interview with Chris in June 2007. More material on the Chris Carmichael story and philosophy can be found at http://www.trainright.com.

111 *cyclist in a wind tunnel:* The article mentioned is Jay T. Kearney, "Training the Olympic Athlete," *Scientific American* 274, 6 (June 1996), p. 52.

114 *"beautiful to see":* Lennard Zinn, "Cadence, Carmichael and Crushing," http://velonews.com/article/1192, July 17, 2001.

117 *completely without branches:* first direct came to my attention when I attended a symposium on customer satisfaction in 1997 and listened to a presentation by Jeffrey Rayport of Harvard Business School. A detailed analysis of first direct can be found in a Harvard Business School case study, number 9-897-079, prepared by Dickson L. Louie under the supervision of Jeffrey F. Rayport, April 9, 1998.

118 *Project Raincloud:* The Project Raincloud task force is discussed in a Harvard Business School case study, number 9-897-079, prepared by Dickson L. Louie under the supervision of Jeffrey F. Rayport, April 9, 1998.

118 *gone to school on Kaizen:* Masaaki Imai, *Kaizen: The Key to Japan's Competitive Success* (McGraw-Hill, 1986). His follow-up book is called *Gemba Kaizen: A Commonsense, Low-Cost Approach to Management* (McGraw-Hill, 1997). Both are excellent treatments of the principles and practices of *Kaizen.*

120 *Taiichi Ohno:* Taiichi Ohno's work and methods can be found in *Toyota Production System: Beyond Large Scale Production* (Productivity Press, 1988).

124 *FAVI . . . short article:* Brian M. Carney, "Workers of Europe Innovate," *Wall Street Journal,* July 25, 2005.

125 *right up front in the conversation:* My interview with Jean-François Zobrist was conducted in March 2008.

127 *how does it work?:* For an in-depth operational analysis of FAVI see Jean Lefebvre and Shoji Shiba, "Collaboration and Trust in the Supply Chain: The Case of FAVI S.A.," *Supply Chain Forum* 6, 2 (2005), pp. 90–95.

132 *Not So Big House:* This section is based on several discussions and interviews with Sarah Susanka during 2007 and 2008, and draws on her several books published by Taunton Press, including *The Not So Big House* (1998), *Creating the Not So Big House* (2000), *Home by Design* (2004), and *Inside the Not So Big House* (2005).

132 *clients of Sarah's:* I met with Sarah Susanka's clients George and Debbie Knopfler, in March 2008, at Lake Sherwood, California.

134 *work of noted architectural design theorist:* Christopher Alexander, *A Pattern Language: Towns, Building, Construction* (Oxford University Press, 1977).

135 *"There is one timeless way":* Christopher Alexander, *A Timeless Way of Building* (Oxford University Press, 1979), p. 5.

135 shibui: Susanka, *Creating the Not So Big House,* p. 38. Sarah e-mailed me this excerpt.

CHAPTER FIVE
*On Sustainable Solutions*

146 double *clay pots:* The story of Mohammed Bah Abba's desert cooler is drawn from two sources: "Low-Tech Solution: Using Simple Physics to Help Poor Nigerians," http://www .rolexawards.com/laureates, and http://www.worldaware.org.uk/ awards.

149 *Star Video:* Barry Nalebuff and Ian Ayres, *Why Not?* (Harvard Business School Press, 2003), pp. 38, 116. It is from this short discussion that the thought exercise is designed.

151 *intuitive shortcutting ability:* The JFK/Hitler exercise is drawn from Morgan D. Jones, *The Thinker's Toolkit* (Three Rivers Press, 1998).

158 *"mental models":* Peter Senge makes a strong case for systems thinking in his seminal book on organizational learning, *The Fifth Discipline* (Doubleday Business, 1990). See also Chris Argyris, *Action Science* (Jossey-Bass, 1985) and *Knowledge for Action* (Jossey-Bass Wiley, 1993).

159 *dramatic loss of market share:* Ian Mitroff's views are found in Senge, *The Fifth Discipline.*

160 *narrow bands of knowledge:* The studies by Stellan Ohlsson of the University of Illinois and Jennifer Wiley of the University of Pittsburgh are discussed in Ulrich Kraft, "Unleashing Creativity," *Scientific American Mind* 16, 1 (2005).

161 *unfocused, or open brainstorming:* See Kevin P. Coyne, Patricia Gorman Clifford, and Renee Dye, "Breakthrough Thinking from Inside the Box," *Harvard Business Review* (December 2007), pp. 71–78.

163 *fixing broken windows:* There are two good profiles of William Bratton: Joe Domanick, "The Reformer, on Honeymoon," *Los Angeles Times Magazine,* January 19, 2003; and Heather Mac Donald, "Chief Bratton Takes on L.A.," *City Journal,* Autumn 2003.

163 *"Broken Windows" theory:* There are four excellent sources on the Broken Windows theory: James Q. Wilson and George L. Kelling, "Broken Windows," *Atlantic Monthly,* March 1982; George L. Kelling and Catherine Coles, *Fixing Broken Windows* (Simon & Schuster/Free Press, 1996); E. J. Dionne, Jr., "A Broken-Windows Approach to Crime," *Washington Post,* December 29, 1996; and Malcolm Gladwell, *The Tipping Point* (Little, Brown & Company, 2000).

169 *Mistress and Maid:* The interesting story of how the NYPD uses art to

improve observational skills came to my attention in the front-page article by Ellen Byron, "New York Officers Learn to Paint Crime Scenes with Broader Strokes," *Wall Street Journal*, July 27, 2005.

170 *very first Lexus:* The most in-depth and inside look at the Lexus story is contained in the book the organization commissioned, *The Lexus Story* (Melcher Media. 2004).

173 *PlayPumps:* The full story of PlayPumps International can be found on the organization's Web site at http://www.playpumps.org. An excellent video exists on their home page.

174 *"The Elephant's Child":* Rudyard Kipling, "The Elephant's Child," *Just So Stories*, 1902; www.kipling.org.uk/poems_serving.htm.

CONCLUSION
## *Elegance in Mind*

177 *Dr. Jeffrey Schwartz:* My second visit with Jeffrey M. Schwartz, M.D., was in April 2008, in Los Angeles, California.

178 *creatives instinctively know:* Ann Emmert Abbott, "The Value of Idle Hours," *Artist's Sketchbook* (October 2004).

179 *New studies . . . creative revelations:* There are two excellent discussions of the Eureka moment: Semir Zeki, "Artistic Creativity and the Brain," *Science* 293 (July 6, 2001), pp. 51–52, and Guenther Knoblich and Michael Oellinger, "The Eureka Moment," *Scientific American Mind* 17, 5 (2006), pp. 38–43.

179 *ultimate break*—sleep: Three good sources on the power of rest in producing creative breakthroughs are Robert Stickgold et al., "Visual Discrimination Learning Requires Sleep After Training," *Nature Neuroscience* 13, 12 (December 2000), pp. 1237–38; Ullrich Wagner et al., "Sleep Inspires Insight," *Nature* 427 (January 22, 2004), pp. 352–55; and Robert Stickgold and Jeffrey Ellenbogen, "Quiet! Sleeping Brain at Work," *Scientific American Mind* 19, 4 (August/September 2008), pp. 22–29.

181 *nonpharmaceutical ways:* Jeffrey Schwartz's book *Brain Lock* (with Beverly Beyette, HarperCollins, 1996) details his work with OCD patients at UCLA. His book with Sharon Begley, *The Mind and the Brain: Neuroplasticity and the Power of Mental Force* (Regan Books, 2003), is considered the authority on the subject of the power of the mind to change the brain.

181 *Buddhist monks, one of the most studied groups:* Sharon Begley, science editor for *Newsweek* and former *Wall Street Journal* science columnist, has written extensively on the studies of Tibetan monks: *Train Your Mind, Change Your Brain* (Ballantine Books, 2007); "How Thinking Can Change the Brain," *Wall Street Journal,* January 19, 2007; and "Scans of Monks' Brains Show Meditation Alters Structure, Functioning," *Wall Street Journal,* November 5, 2004.

182 *mindful awareness meditation:* Jeff Schwartz's directions for mindful meditation originally appeared in his book *Dear Patrick* (Harper Perennial, 2003), 174–75.

184 *origins of insight:* The work of Mark Jung-Beeman can be gleaned from three good sources, one academic and the others popular: Mark Jung-Beeman and John Kounios et al., "The Origins of Insight in Resting-State Brain Activity," *Neuropsychologia* 46 (2008); Jonah Lehrer, "The Eureka Hunt," *New Yorker,* July 28, 2008; and "Scientists Explain 'Aha!' Moments: Brain Activity Differs When Creative Insight Takes Hold," WebMD Health, News, available at http://men.webmd.com/news/20040413/scientists-explain-aha-moments.

185 *testing out BrainPaint:* My meetings, discussions, interviews, and sessions with Bill Scott at BrainPaint were conducted in April and May 2008 in Los Angeles, California.

187 *laboratory study:* Tobias Egner and John Gruzelier, "Ecological Validity of Neurofeedback: Modulation of Slow Wave EEG Enhances Musical Performance," *Cognitive Neuroscience and Neuropsychology* 14, 9 (July 2003).

# *Index*

(Page numbers in italics indicate illustrations.)